GUIDE to ARTISTS
IN SOUTHERN CALIFORNIA

GUIDE to ARTISTS IN SOUTHERN CALIFORNIA

Compiled and edited by Vanessa Obten

Foreword by Henry T. Hopkins
Chair, UCLA Art Department
Director, UCLA at the
Armand Hammer Museum of Art and Cultural Center

ART Resource Publications
Santa Monica, California

Publisher's Cataloging-in-Publication Data

Obten, Vanessa
Guide to artists in Southern California / Vanessa Obten.
p. cm.
Includes index.
Preassigned LCCN: 94-78159
ISBN 0-9642995-0-X

1. Artists--California, Southern--Catalogs. 2. Art, American--California, Southern--Catalogs. 3. Artists--California, Southern--Directories. 4. Art, Modern--20th century--California, Southern--Catalogs. I. Title.

N6530.S72028 1995 709.794'904
QBI94-1863

Guide to Artists in Southern California is offered as an information source only. A listing does not constitute endorsement by the publisher.

Cover design by **Sheldon Seidler**
Cover photographs by **Pamela Leeds**

Cover artists: **Dawn Arrowsmith, Brad Durham, Linda Yaven Echeverria and Jim Morphesis**

Printed in Hong Kong

ART Resource Publications

2118 Wilshire Boulevard., Suite 131, Santa Monica, CA 90403

For Jason with love

Acknowledgements

My thanks go first to my dear friend Shel: without his encouragement and his help this project never would have been realized.

Thanks also to Pam for providing the access route and, along with Richard, some very well chosen words. To Hal for keeping me laughing and for getting me on balance and to Stuart for helping to keep me there. To Jeff for being first. To Dawn, Elaine, Linda, Lisa and John for their recommendations and help. To James for all the words, written, read and spoken and especially for the Sermon. To Martin for always being willing to answer my questions. To Ellen for her ideas and comments. To Laurel for help in editing. To Ann for all her help at the critical hour. To Maddy and Gary, Carol and Fred, Phyllis, Bonnie, Doug, and Ron. To John, who was there encouraging me at the very beginning. Thank you and love to you all.

Thank you to Florence Janovic and Judith Appelbaum for their continued ideas, help and support.

And a very special thanks to the wonderful community of artists in Southern California.

Contents

Foreword

Nothing Ventured, Nothing Gained

This is a time when the traditional support mechanisms for the visual arts — galleries, alternative spaces and museums — are no longer sufficient to serve the growing number and needs of artists working in the Los Angeles area. For this reason, inventive people need to find new methods to develop and maintain contacts between the art-interested and the art makers.

Guide to Artists in Southern California, the brainchild of Vanessa Obten, is an intelligent communicating device and merchandising mechanism which takes an important step in this direction. The Guide, in its first edition, provides excellent information about a large number of artists in our community, as well as providing the art-aware public with a tool for approaching these artists in their studios on a one-to-one basis without having to go through an often costly middleman.

One can only hope that the Guide will have the salutary effect of bringing the artist and his/her audience into humane contact.

Henry T. Hopkins
Chair, UCLA Art Department
Director, UCLA at the Armand Hammer
Museum of Art and Cultural Center

How to Use the Guide

Going to the Source

This Guide introduces some of the finest artists in Southern California and offers access to their studios.

Its pages present a diverse cross-section of the rich and varied Southern California art scene. The artists included range from avant-garde to traditional and work in a broad range of media and styles. Some are already internationally recognized; others are emerging.

To present each artist as vividly as possible, the Guide presents text that the artists themselves have created along with black and white illustrations of their work. The majority of these illustrations reproduce originals that are in full color.

Examples of work by several of the artists also appear in a color folio, arranged alphabetically by the artist's name. The second page number after an artist's name in the Artist Index and Index by Media at the back of the Guide refers to his/her color illustration.

You have an open invitation to visit these artists' studios, provided only that you follow these few simple guidelines:

- If the artist's entry says, *Studio visits by appointment,* do not arrive unannounced; telephone first, preferably several days in advance, to arrange a mutually convenient time. And be sure to call if you must cancel or reschedule.
- Check for current addresses of artists, museums and galleries before visiting. Although we've made every effort to provide accurate, up-to-date information, facts may have changed since the Guide went to press.

The Guide is your introduction to these artists and their art and will enable you to take home, live with and enjoy some of the best work being done in America today.

Vanessa Obten

Diane Destiny

Painting

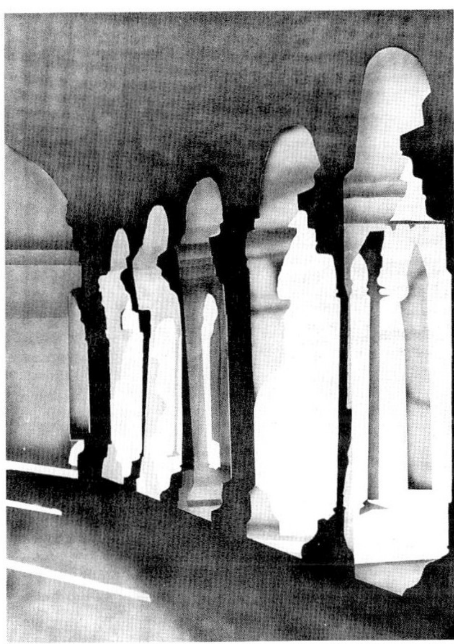

Cloisters, airbrush on aluminum, 3 x 4'

Artist, lecturer and educator, Diane Destiny has been exhibiting nationally since 1970. Having mastered several bodies of work in various exotic media, including a series of hi-tech constructions and small works in Braille, she is currently involved with the application of transparent inks to an aluminum ground.

Destiny is a world traveler who spends extended periods of time in each locale photographing fragments of that culture. Later, in her studio, having made selections from her photographs, she abstracts her images by airbrushing vibrant colors onto the highly-tooled aluminum bases. The effect is quasi-impressionistic. However, she ventures far beyond that genre.

The finished pieces are unframed and float out from the wall. Such strategies together with the magical glints of light that flicker kinetically across the surfaces, expand the dimensions of the works conceptually into the surrounding spaces. Ever investigative, yet substantive, her work exudes a consummate beauty that reflects her deeply sincere appreciation of the life around us.

Commissions accepted.

Studio visits by appointment: (818) 791-4541. Destiny's studio is located at 29 West Silver Spruce Lane, Altadena, CA 91001.

Diane Holland

Prints (electrotransfer)

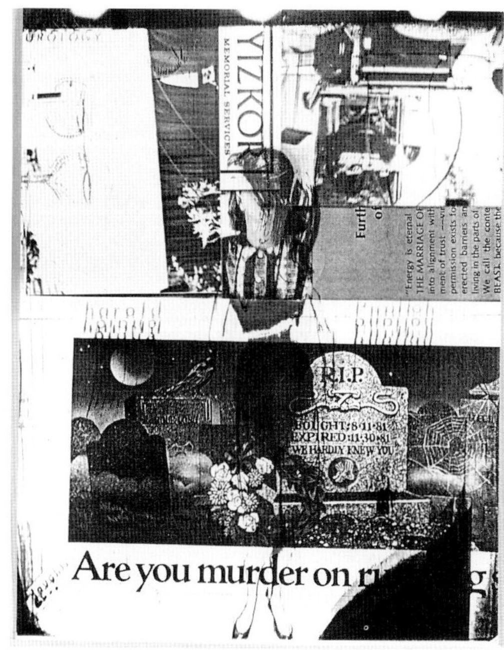

Somatic Telesthesia, B.3
electrotransfer on paper
11 x 8 1/2"

I use electrotransfer (that is, color xerography) and Cibachrome photography to interpret and convey the relationship that develops between human beings and the technological artifacts they create. The series of images entitled *Somatic Telesthesia* focuses on the kinds of technological interactions that impact upon the individual on both a personal and a cultural level. The source material for electrostatic and photographic composite alike is drawn from real and imagined experience. Ultimately, the composites are meant to function as vehicles for personal awareness and social change. — Diane Holland

Diane Holland, who received a B.A. (with honors) at Immaculate Heart College and her M.F.A. at the Otis/Parsons School (now the Otis College) of Art and Design, has exhibited in numerous thematic exhibitions in California and elsewhere. She has also created and participated in many performances, and maintains a parallel career as a screen and television actress.

Commissions accepted.

Holland's work can be seen at Couturier Gallery, Los Angeles, (213) 933-5557, and William Turner Gallery, Venice, (310) 392-8399.

Studio visits by appointment: (213) 655-9914.

Karen Fuson

Sculpture

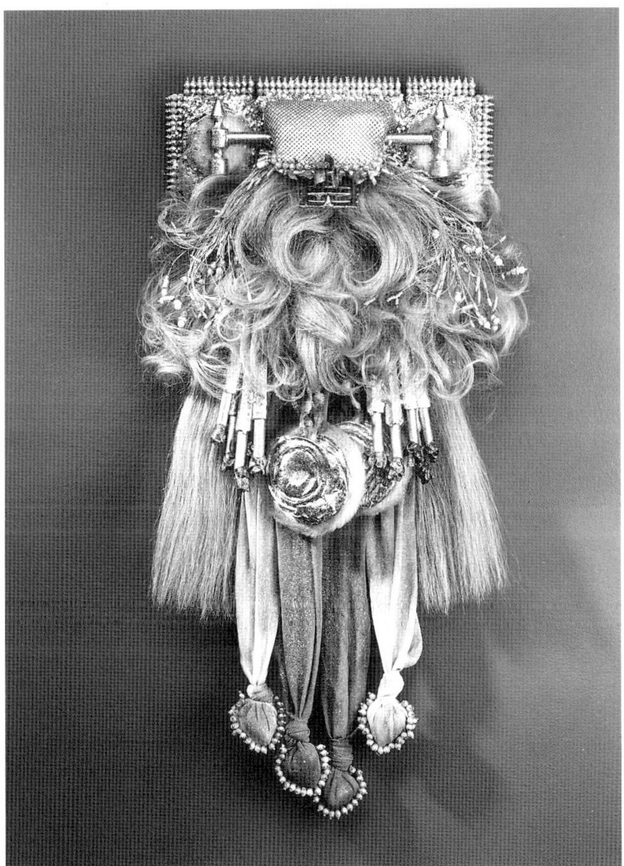

Hammerhead, Votary XXII, mixed media on wood/assemblage 25 1/2 x 15 x 4 1/2". Photo: David Spellman

My work, from 1982 to the present, has centered on the investigation of the feminine principle, ideals of female beauty and body image, and gender role stereotypes. While my assemblages symbolize the power invested in accessorized, merchandised "beauty," my intention in transmogrifying cultural artifacts is to subvert popular expectations of ideal beauty. — Karen Fuson

Fuson's work can be seen at Roy G. Biv Fine Art, Palm Springs (619) 864-7200 and Patricia Correia Gallery, Venice (310) 314-2626.

Studio visits by appointment. Call for address and directions: (714) 754-7023.

Marlene Louchheim

Sculpture

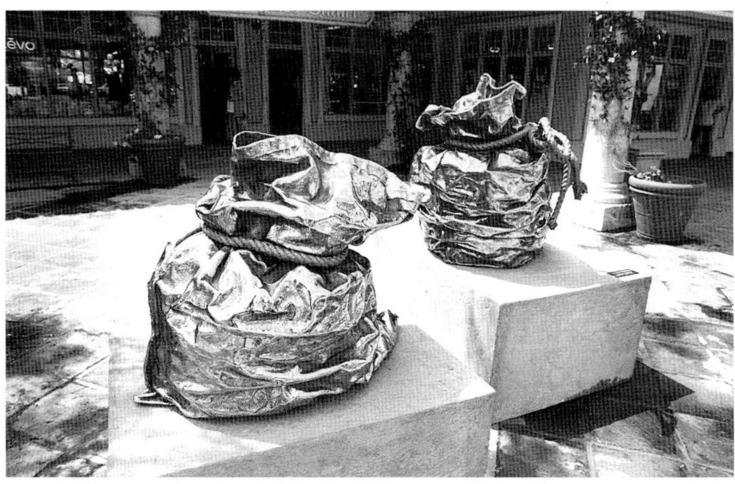

Standing Together, burlap and polished bronze
left 42 1/2 x 48 x 33", right 42 x 53 x 31"

Marlene Louchheim's burlap sculptures talk to each other. They talk about love, about distance, about fear and tenderness. They laugh, they struggle and they mourn. Known best for her "Bag Series," Louchheim uses burlap, bronze, aluminum and copper to create an emotional stage for the natural twists and sensual curves found in the material.

Throughout her life she has been an observer of relationships, always intrigued with the subtleties within our expression to one another. The burlap becomes an unending investigation into the possibilities of this dance. Through the "Bag Series," and through her wall reliefs, she has taken this fascination with communication to a place of deep respect and grace.

Louchheim's sculptures range in size from small, intimate indoor pieces which can either be hung or placed, to large outdoor pieces. Her work is shown widely and collected by many private individuals and corporations.

Media: Burlap, bronze, aluminum, copper and resin.

Commissions accepted. Prices available upon request.

Her work can be seen through Carl Schlosberg Fine Art, Sherman Oaks, (818) 783-6209.

Studio visits by appointment: (310) 558-4125, (310) 275-2762. Marlene Louchheim Studio is located at 8743 B West Washington Boulevard, Culver City CA 90232.

David Silverman

Sculpture

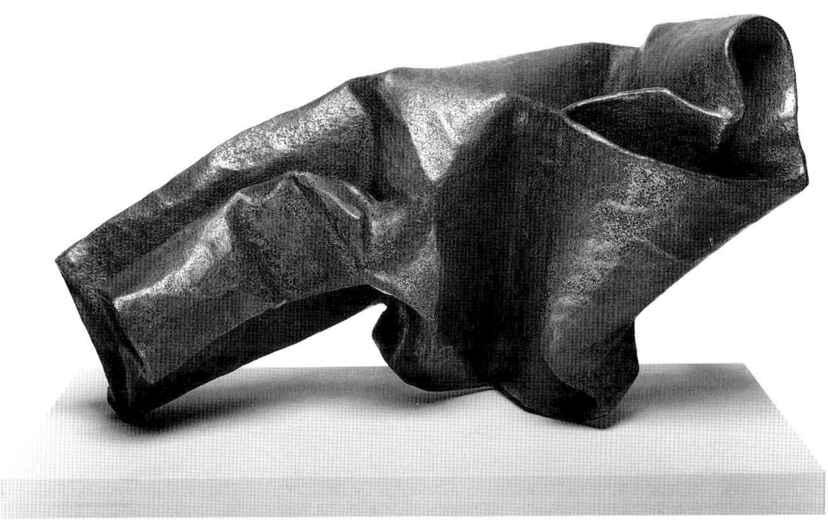

Torso, bronze, 30 x 11 x 15 1/2". Photo Brian Forrest

David Silverman imposes human sensitivity on pre-formed industrial paper cylinders, creating a synthesis of geometric and organic shapes. He dis-organizes and re-organizes them before coating them with a thick molten metal spray. The result is forms that become fluid.

Media: Bronze, aluminum, copper, brass

Commissions accepted.

Visits to Silverman's studio, Sycamore Studio, are by appointment: (310) 826-5003, (310) 392-2697.

Walter Gabrielson

Wall Sculpture / Painting

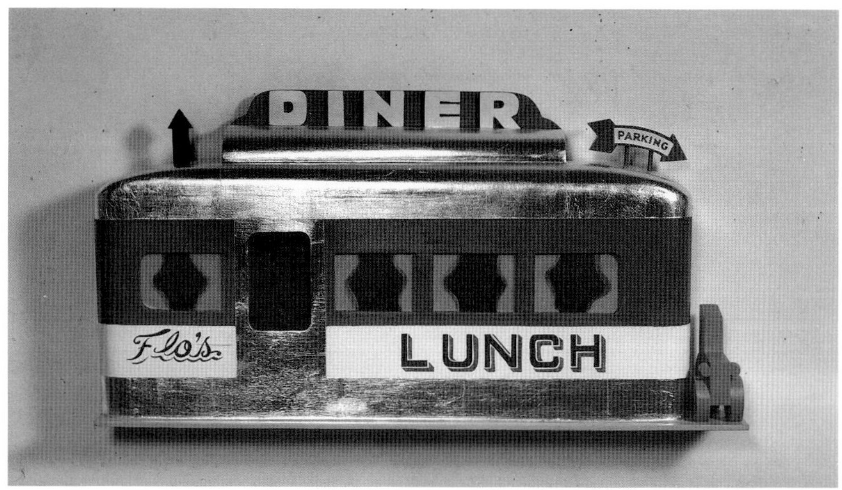

Flo's Lunch (wall piece), painted wood,12 1/2 x 24 x 4"

Walter Gabrielson makes wry, whimsical wall pieces reflective of California lifestyles. The works are interplays between a character and a set, which might be a diner, old movie, hot dog stand, country store, big donut drive-in or the last gas station out in the desert. They include humorous views of the professions, as in *The Deposition*, and the operating room, *You May Experience Some Discomfort*. Paintings of these scenes are also available. According to *The Los Angeles Times*, "one of our canniest social observers and wittiest commentators, Gabrielson is an expressionist who heightens emotion with exaggerated gestures and seductive color."

Media: Painted wood, oil on canvas.

Commissions accepted. Major painting commission can be viewed at the Hilton Hotel near the Burbank Airport.

Prices are from $600 wholesale for small wall pieces (about 26" high) and then dependent upon size and complexity.

Gabrielson's work can be viewed at Brushworks in San Diego, (619) 232-7329 and Steve Stein Gallery in Sherman Oaks, (818) 990-0777, and Montecito, (805) 565-2032.

Studio visits by appointment: (805) 683-4761. His studio is located at 375 Pine Avenue, #2, Goleta, CA 93117.

David Collis

Painting

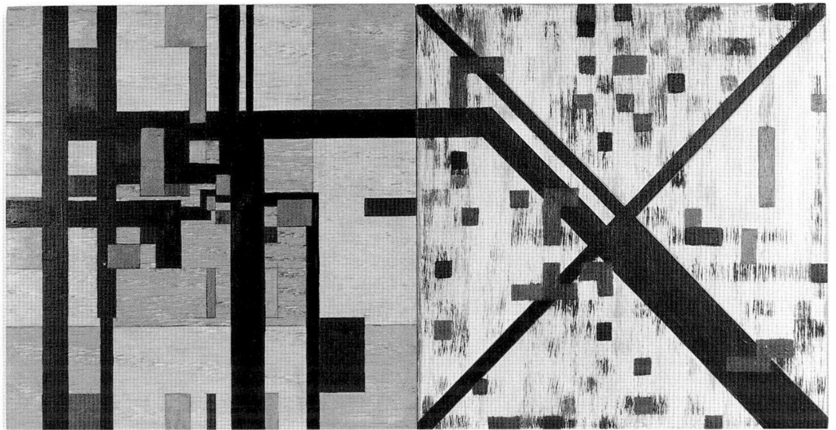

Segments #2, acrylic on wood, 8 x 16". Photo: Christian Mounger

The nature of my work is connected to art history and the process of painting. I connect with the history of art by employing art historical movements and writing within a systematized method to create shape, pattern, color and line. My involvement is to set up a binary relationship between a rational system of a pre-determined set of grids and the chance placement of color blocks and random lines. Each window of the grid is numbered. The placement of the color blocks and the lines are directly linked to the numbered windows. The collusion of these two distinct systems produce the work. My hand only helps it to materialize --David Collis

Commissions accepted.

Studio visits by appointment: (310) 376-3955. David Collis Studios is located at 2919 Hermosa View Drive, Hermosa Beach, CA, 90254

Judy Chan

Mixed Media

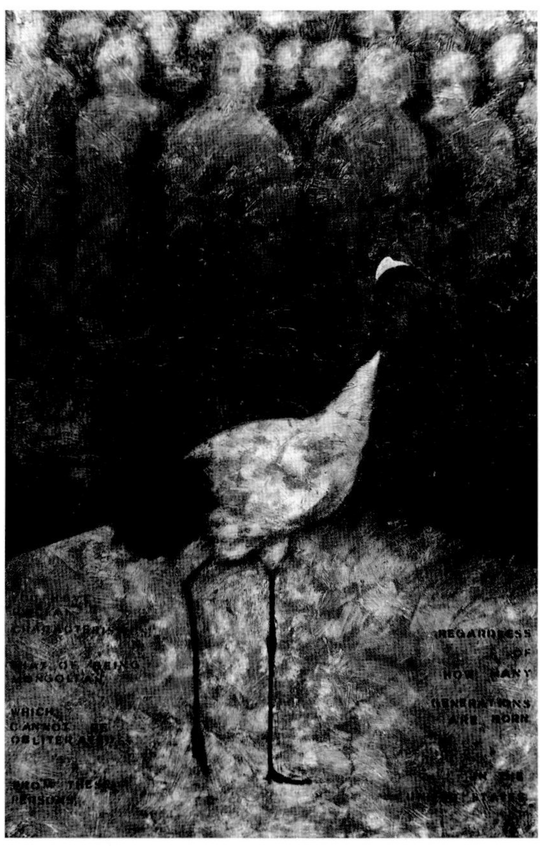

Do I Have to Be the Enemy #3, oil on paper, 60 x 40"

Do *I Have to Be the Enemy #3* is part of an installation of seven oil paintings on rag paper, free-standing, three-dimensional objects, and quotations taken from a Congressional hearing held in 1942. The installation is about the internment of American-Japanese during World War II.

As an American-Japanese, my work is about my experiences and thoughts which I use as a catalyst to create images, utilizing symbolism, in a semi-abstract style. — Judy Chan

Media: Mixed-media drawings, paintings with 3-dimensional objects attached, fiber sculptures and monotypes.

Education: M.F.A. in Printmaking from Cal State Long Beach

Commissions accepted.

Call for appointment, address and directions: (310) 428-7786.

Peter Zokosky

Painting

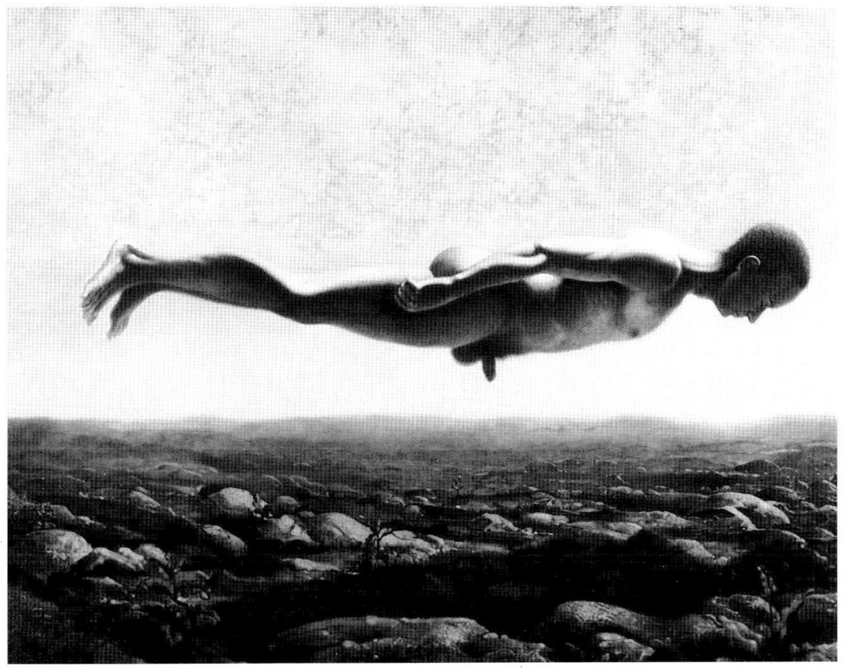

Gravity, oil on canvas, 28 1/4 x 41"

Commissions considered.

Studio visits by appointment: (310) 498-8334.

Leslie Schumann

Assemblage

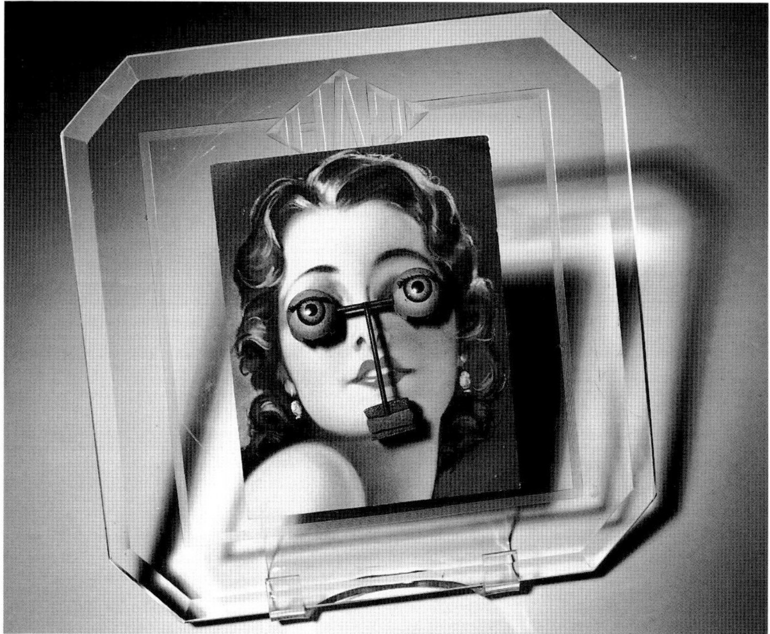

Hollywood Daze, assemblage/artifacts, 8 x 8". Photo: Michael Stern

I am a child of an inventor and sculptor.
I am a child of the '60s.
I am a child of psychoanalysis.
I am a child of surrealism

I resonate to Andre Breton's words in his *Manifeste du Surrealisme* (1924), wherein he "struck up an enthusiastic hymn to imagination, the fountain where (people) could find eternal youth, and denounced adults for having let the passage of time rob them of a child's faculty of playfulness."

Breton defined Surrealism as "the spontaneous exploitation of 'pure psychic automatism,' allowing the production of an abundance of unexpected images." His followers "affirmed the rights of the dream, of love, of awareness and they joined in encouraging the mind to be open to wild encounters and to the surprises afforded by chance." They saw life as a "poetic adventure."— Leslie Schuman child/child therapist/artist

She has exhibited her work both in Paris and the U.S.

Media: Assemblage, found objects, artifacts.

Studio visits by appointment: (213) 223-0369.

Cynthia Burgess

Mixed Media

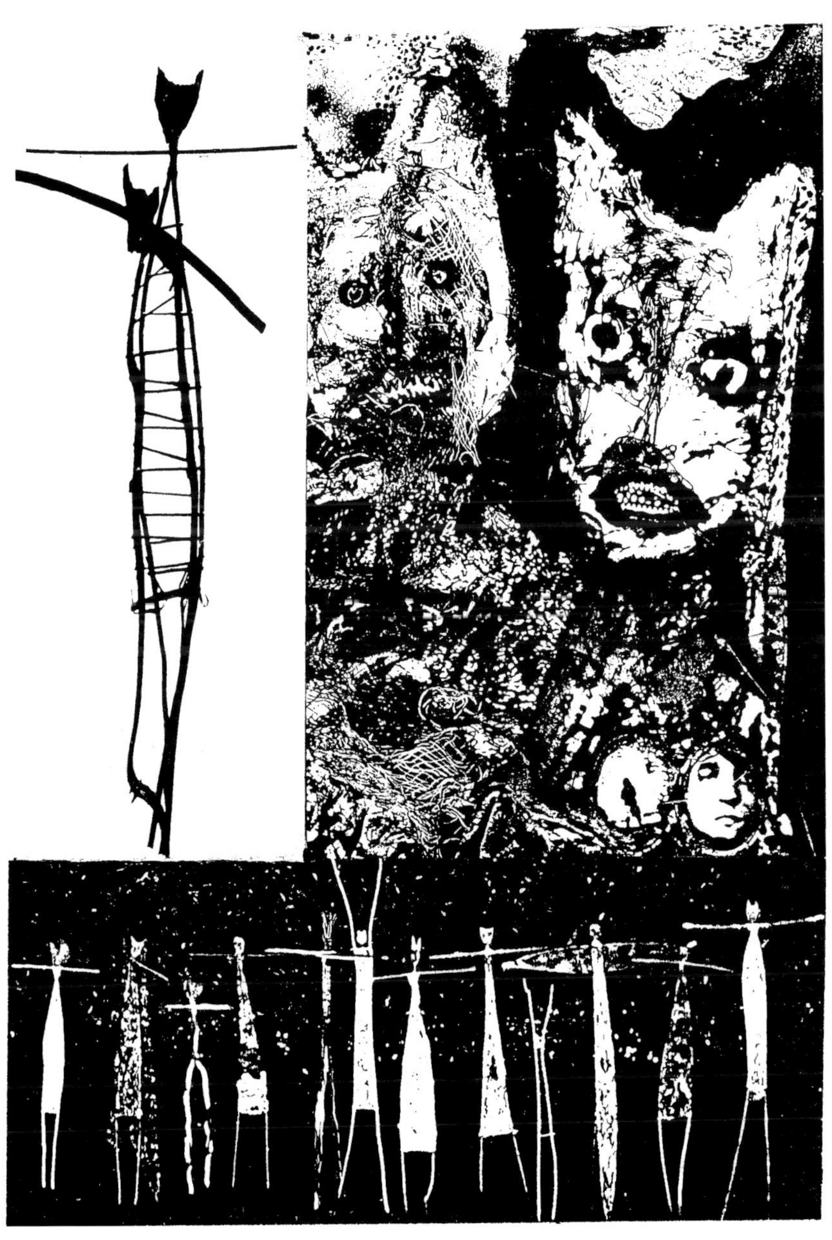

Studio visits by appointment: (310) 477-9764.

Judi Donin

Mixed Media / Jewelry

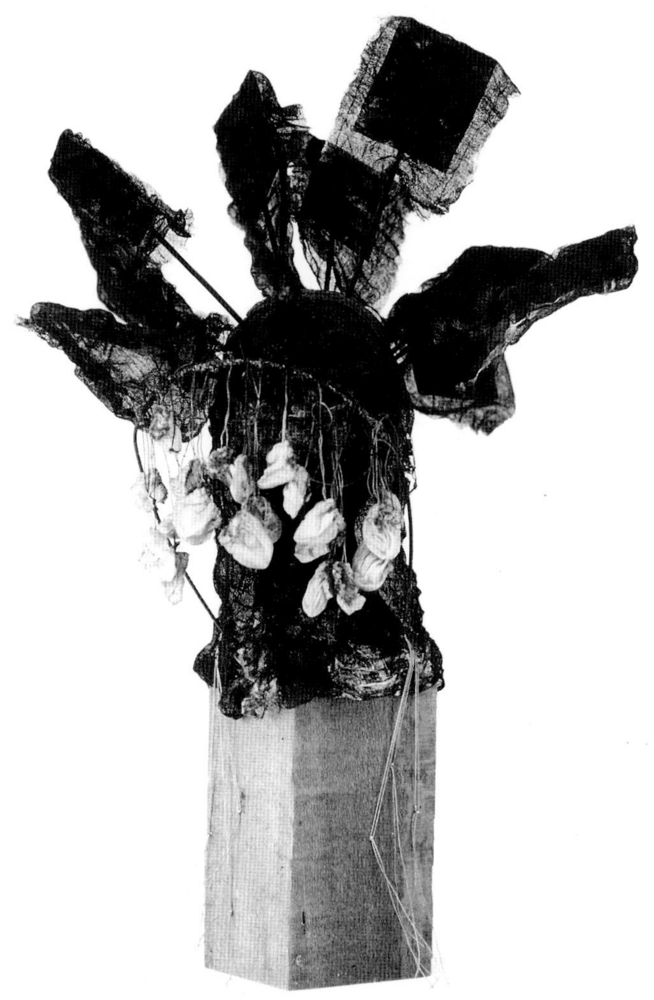

Points of View / Points of You, mixed media, 28 x 16 x 19"

Commissions accepted.

Donin's work in jewelry can be seen at the Museum of Contemporary Art (MOCA) Store, Los Angeles (213) 621-1710.

Studio visits by appointment: (310) 659-4344, Donin's studio is located at 645 Westmount Drive, #212, Los Angeles, CA 90069.

Lisa Adams

Painting / Sculpture

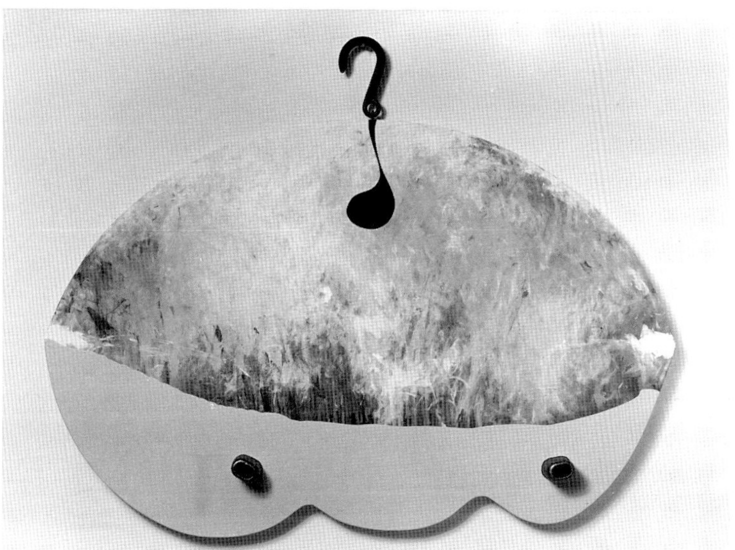

Frogy!, acrylic and steel on wood, 40 x 42". Photo: Gene Ogami

Through a shifting combination of shaped surfaces, inclusion of industrial materials and impulsive application of muted and solid colors, [Adams] defies conventional pigeon-holing of stylistic innovations and derivations. — Mat Gleason, *Coagula*

Adams works very much in the tradition of abstract painting. Like most interesting artists of her generation pursuing this direction, she has avoided the limiting dogmas of formalist theory to embrace an inclusive attitude more reminiscent of early modernism . . . Adams' concerns are more directed toward a complex visual and conceptual dialogue. Her art can therefore be experienced on multiple levels. — David DiMichele, *Visions Magazine*

. . . Adams' work, equally rooted in sculpture and painting, kindles a palpable sense of private examination, the turning of the light back toward the source. — Miles Beller, *Artweek*

Her work is included in many corporate, public and private collections including Edward Albee Foundation, Montauk, NY; Eli Broad Foundation, Los Angeles; and Nippon Steel USA, Inc., Los Angeles.

Commissions accepted.

Studio visits by appointment: (213) 623-7266. Adams' studio is located at 2118 East 7th Place, Los Angeles, CA, 90021.

Dawn Arrowsmith

Painting

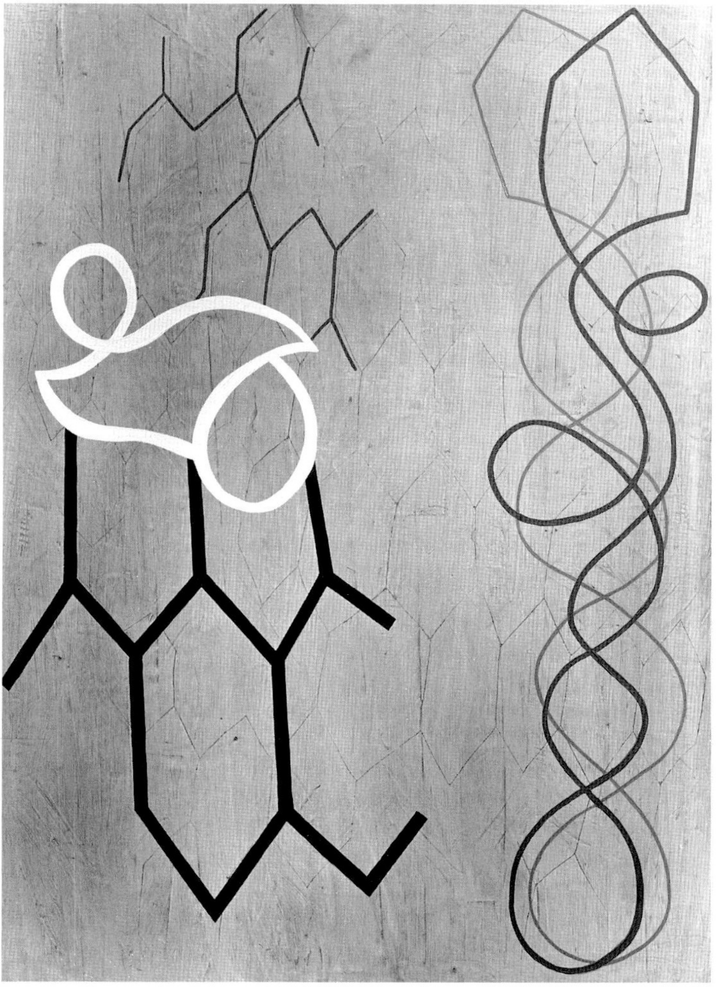

Second Look, oil on wood panel, 42 x 32". Photo: Gene Ogami

Dawn Arrowsmith has exhibited nationally and internationally for the past 10 years. Her small to large scale paintings, bas reliefs and sculptures continue to deal with an enduring intimacy between woman and nature. Her work has been placed in public, corporate and private collections.

Slides and prices available on request.

Studio visits by appointment: (213) 585-1785.

Pat Berger

Painting

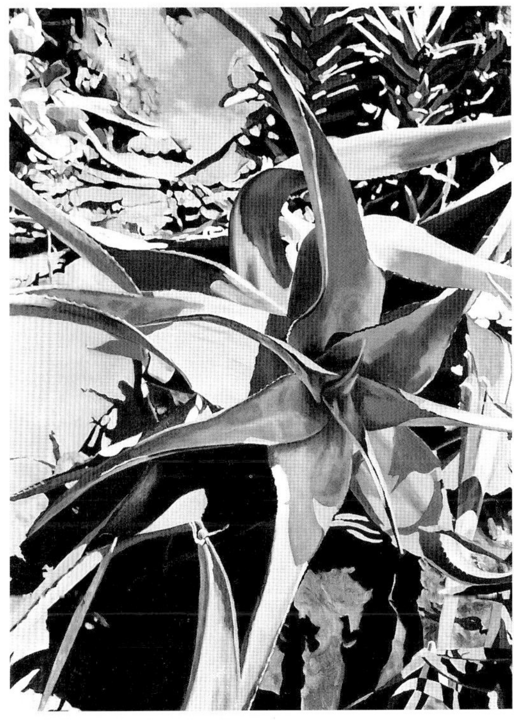

Century Plant
acrylic on canvas
60 x 48"
Photo: American Photocopy

Pat Berger has become known for her paintings depicting the homeless in our cities. Another aspect of her work deals with plant life. The play of shadows combined with close-up sections of the plants create bold and compelling images that are at once realistic, yet abstract. They become a world of their own.

Berger's work is represented in many museum, corporate and private collections. Her awards include purchase awards from the Ford Foundation, Watercolor USA, and West Art and the Law. Her paintings range in size from murals and large scale paintings to smaller intimate pieces.

Media: Acrylic, watercolor, oil sticks, monotypes

Commissions accepted.

Berger's work can be seen at Valerie Miller Fine Art, Palm Desert, (619) 773-4483; Landau/20th Century Art, Los Angeles, (310) 474-5155; and Adelle M. Fine Art, Dallas, TX, (214) 220-0300.

Studio visits by appointment. Call for address and directions: (310) 838-8346.

Alan Blizzárd

Painting

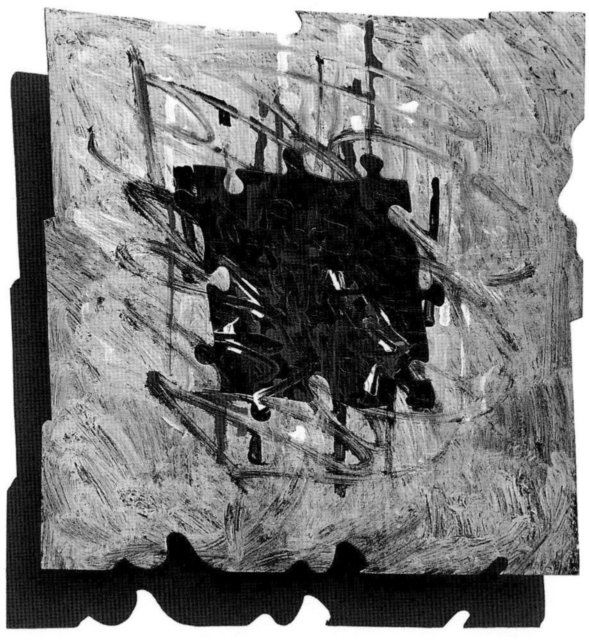

Broken Arrow #13, rhoplex on canvas and wood, 24 x 24"

Alan Blizzárd is a painter's painter. His work is dedicated to the toughest aesthetic standards and excellence of craft.

As with the finest painters, Blizzárd's art functions within a sensitive balance of will and intellect. Structure and spatialism perform on the *tabula rasa.*

Blizzárd believes that the contemporary painter must protect against subsummation by momentary electronic space fills, sound bytes and pixels. He feels that art is art and entertainment is everything else. Experiencing painting requires space, time and solitude, all of which are endangered entities.

Blizzárd's paintings have been shown and collected widely throughout Europe, Canada, and the U.S. He is represented in numerous public and private collections including: Art Institute of Chicago, Denver Art Museum, Columbia University, Fluor Corporation and the Kouri Capital Corporation of New York City.

Blizzárd is a professor of painting at Scripps College.

Studio visits by appointment: (213) 588-4162.

Robbie Conal

Painting

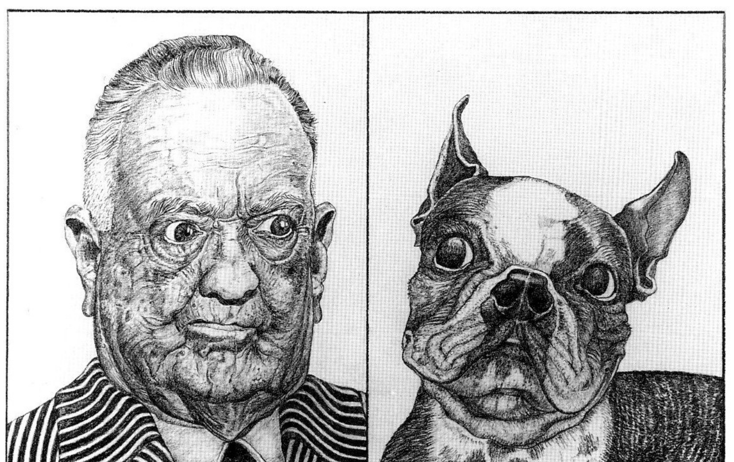

Pet Peeve (J. Edgar Hoover & his Boston Terrier), graphite on paper, 23 x 29"

I grew up as an "art brat" in New York City (on the "upper left side"). My brat pack friends and I got kicked out of every major museum and every public library in town. I got psychedelicized at San Francisco State University in the '60s (did a double major in hallucinogenic drugs and cafeteria coffee). Then I got professionalized at Stanford University in the '70s. When I moved to Los Angeles in the '80s, encroaching adulthood forced me to integrate my personality —put my art and my social concerns together — and finally make pictures about subjects that were important to me: Politics, Power, and the abuses of both. I quickly realized that art institutions are a very limited arena of reception for ideas about public issues, so I translated my original paintings and drawings into posters and ran around the streets like a midnight maniac, splattering glue in every major American city I could get to on my no budget, non-scheduled, total loss, rock'n'roll poster tours . . . building up a volunteer guerrilla postering army as I went. My art is a form of non-sanctioned counter-infotainment. If I can get people to think along with me about issues I think are important and provide them with a little surprise on their way to work in the morning, I'm happy. — Robbie Conal

Commissions accepted.

Conal's work can be seen at Koplin Gallery, Santa Monica, (310) 319-9956; and Jayne H. Baum Gallery, New York, NY, (212) 219-9854.

Studio visits by appointment: (310) 915-0774.

Katherine Coons

Painting / Sculpture

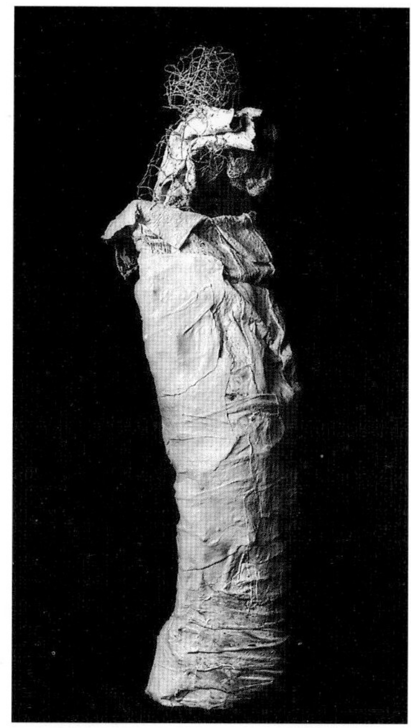

Standing Shroud
plaster, cloth and wire
64 x 20 x 20"
Photo: Scott Hensel

Coons' philosophy about making art expresses the process of *doing*, coupled with intuitive thought. The nature of her work evolves from theories on aesthetics.

"It is important for the artist to remain 'centered' in the studio by maintaining a constant reassessment and openness toward change. My work has grown into a style I term abstract-figuration which is neither figurative nor fully abstract. The palette is darker and the surface more spatial. While many of the subjects are indistinguishable and the figures diluted, the motive is to keep the images moving so they are constantly readjusting themselves." — Katherine Coons

Solo exhibits include The Brand Art Library in Glendale, Cal Poly Pomona, EZTV and The Senior Eye Gallery in Long Beach. Group exhibits include the Los Angeles County Museum of Art, Artspace Gallery and The Directors Guild of America.

Coons studied at the Sorbonne, Paris, France and The Université de Tours, Tours France under Rutgers University.

Commissions accepted.

Studio visits by appointment: (213) 680-9733. Coon's studio is located at 201 South Santa Fe Avenue, Studio 207, Los Angeles, CA 90012.

David DiMichele

Painting

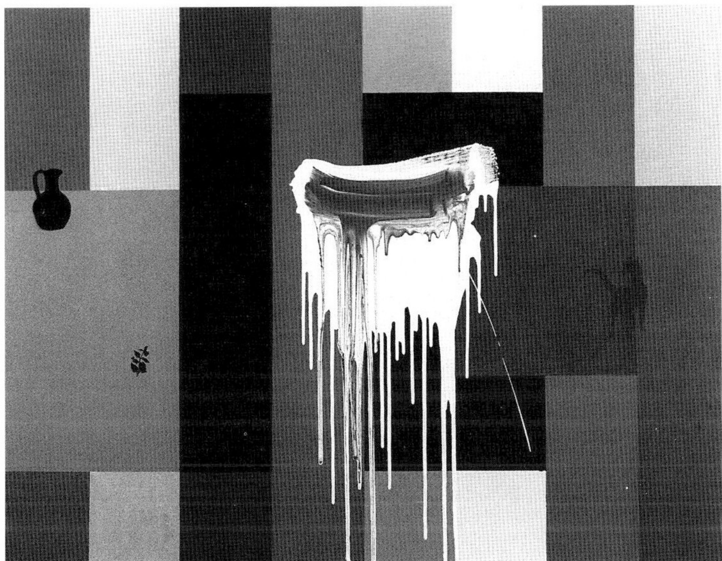

The Decline of the God-Kings, oil on canvas, 36 x 48"

. . . DiMichele conflates the idea of Color Field Painting with the subjectivity of Abstract Expressionism and, for good measure, makes a philosophical inquiry a la Wittgenstein into the nature of word and image. In short, the piece functions as a sort of Post-Conceptual Dictionary of Appropriated Abstraction. — James Scarborough, *Art Press Magazine*

DiMichele's work relates to a group of contemporary Los Angeles painters that are exploring the terrain between formalism and signs/symbols. — Boulton Colburn, Curator of Collections, Laguna Art Museum

Brilliant and Humorous. — Mat Gleason, *Coagula*

Los Angeles artist, David DiMichele, creates paintings that address the viability of non-objective art within a post-modern, post-formalist environment. His work has been featured in several recent exhibitions that explore new directions in abstract painting, including *The Cultivated Field, Almost Monochrome,* and *Uncooperative Abstraction*. He is represented in many public and private collections, including Bank of America, Reebok and Disney corporations, and by a major work, *Mental Abilities,* at the Laguna Art Museum.

Studio visits by appointment: (213) 626-3887.

James Doolin

Painting

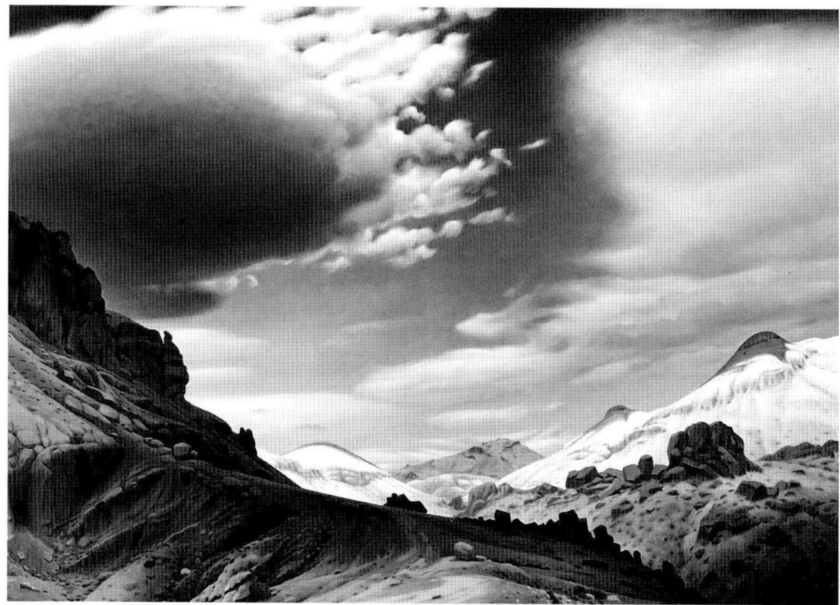

Primal Landscape, oil on canvas, 72 x 102". Courtesy of Koplin Gallery
Photo: Brewer Photography

For more than 25 years, James Doolin has made large-scale paintings and smaller plein-air paintings of both the urban and natural landscape in Southern California. His paintings are known for their intense observation of light, color and space, and they can be seen as an homage to both the poetics of our physical surroundings and the wonder of visual experience itself. He is represented in public, corporate and private collections throughout the United States and Australia.

Commissions accepted. Price estimates upon request.

Doolin's work can be seen at Koplin Gallery, Santa Monica, (310) 319-9956; and Stremmel Gallery, Reno, NV, (702) 786-0558.

Studio visits by appointment. Call for address and directions: (310) 559-6263.

Brad Durham

Painting

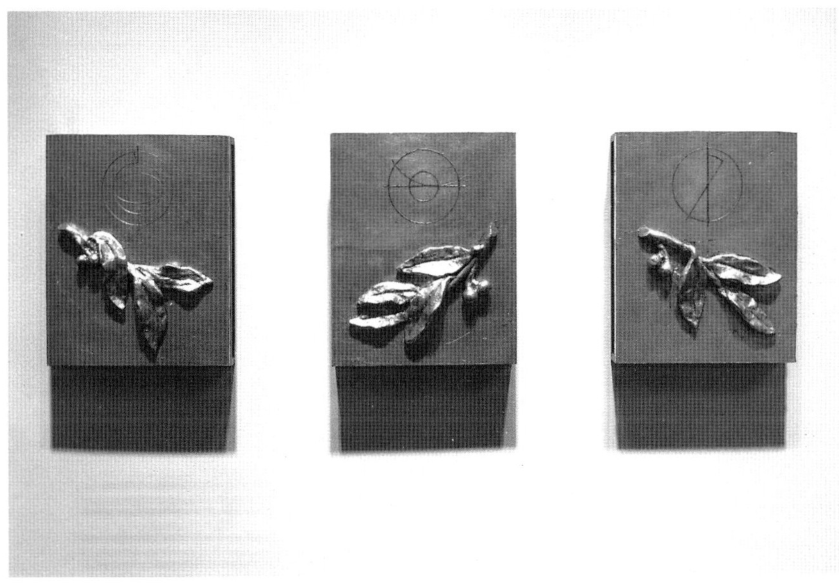

Form No. 1-3, 11 x 9 x 3 1/2" each, oil on gold leaf on bronze

Studio visits by appointment: (213) 222-9398. Durham's studio is located at 629 Moulton Avenue, Studio B, Los Angeles, CA 90031.

Gregory Wiley Edwards

Painting

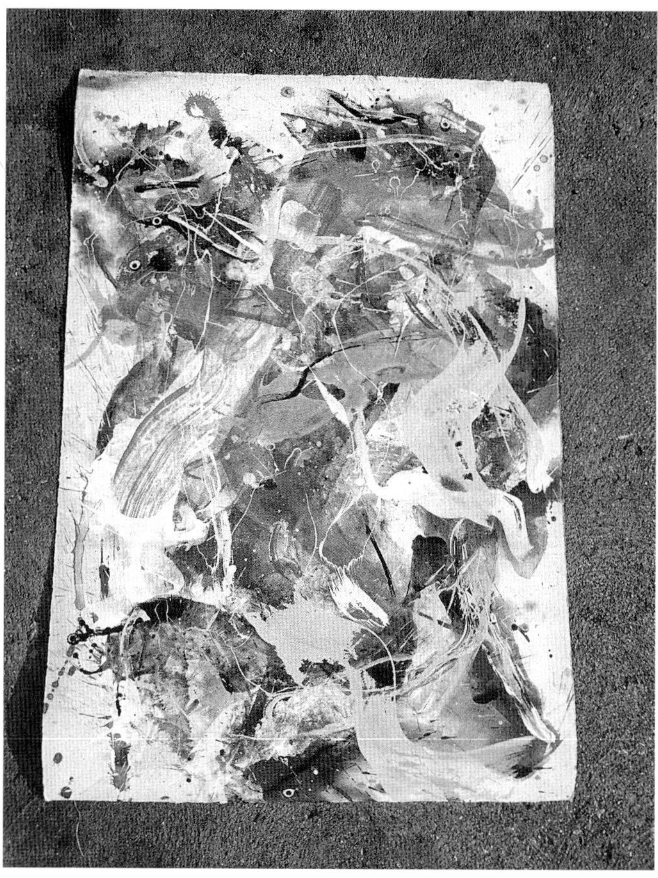

Under Ground, acrylic on paper, 41 3/4 x 27 1/2"

Gregory Edwards is a post-modern abstract painter. The aim of his work is to contribute to the ascendency of his spirit. He finds influences locally, in this era and globally — back into antiquity. The work is informed by the wisdom of Africa, Native Americas and Asia as well as that of Europe. The methods he employs are spontaneous and diverse to better address the needs of his specific aesthetic purpose — the raising of consciousness.

Commissions accepted.

Edwards' work can be seen at Brian Gross Gallery, San Francisco (415) 788-1050 and Valerie Miller Fine Arts, Palm Desert (619) 773-4483.

Studio visits by appointment: (213) 662-0783.

Janne M. Greibesland

Painting

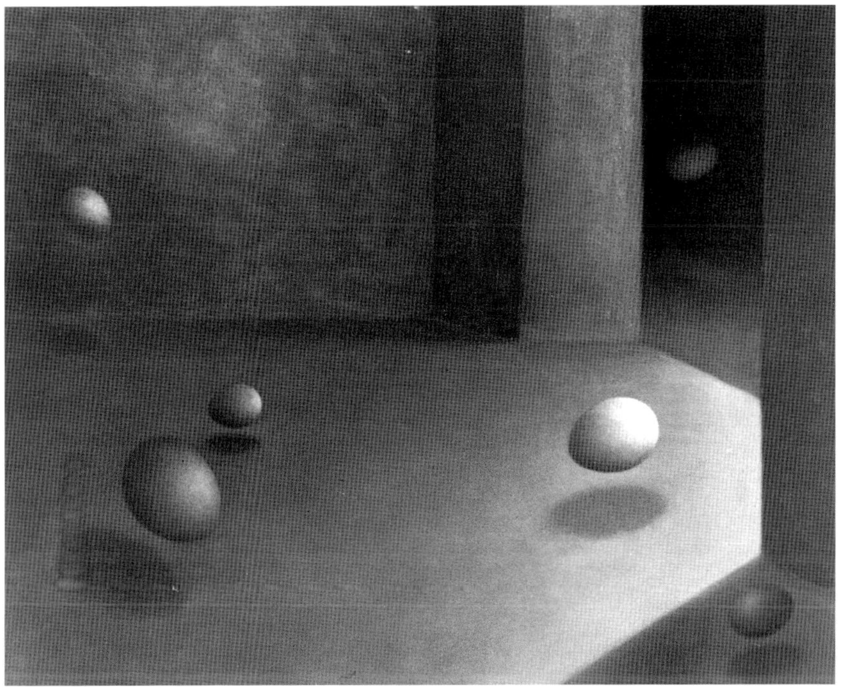

Visitors from the Void, paper, acrylic and oil on canvas, 6 1/2 x 8 1/2'

Janne M. Greibesland studied art in both Italy and her native Norway. Her work is included in collections in Germany, Italy, Norway and the U.S.

Commissions accepted.

Studio visits by appointment: (213) 467- 5240

Ariel Heart

Painting

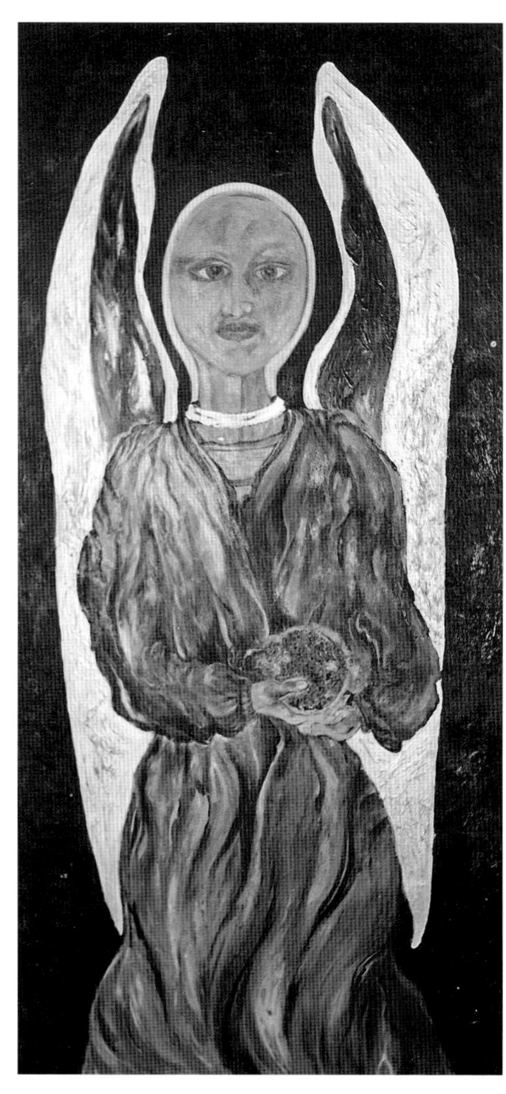

Lilith
mixed media on canvas
8 x 4'
Photo: Gary Silk

Commissions accepted.

Heart's paintings can be seen at Installations One Gallery, Encino, (818) 981-9422. Works on paper are available at Print Merchants, Pacific Design Center, Los Angeles, (310) 659-9260.

Studio visits by appointment: (213) 660-1599. Her studio, Studio 2000, is located at 2000 Talmadge Street, Los Angeles, CA 90027.

F. Scott Hess

Painting

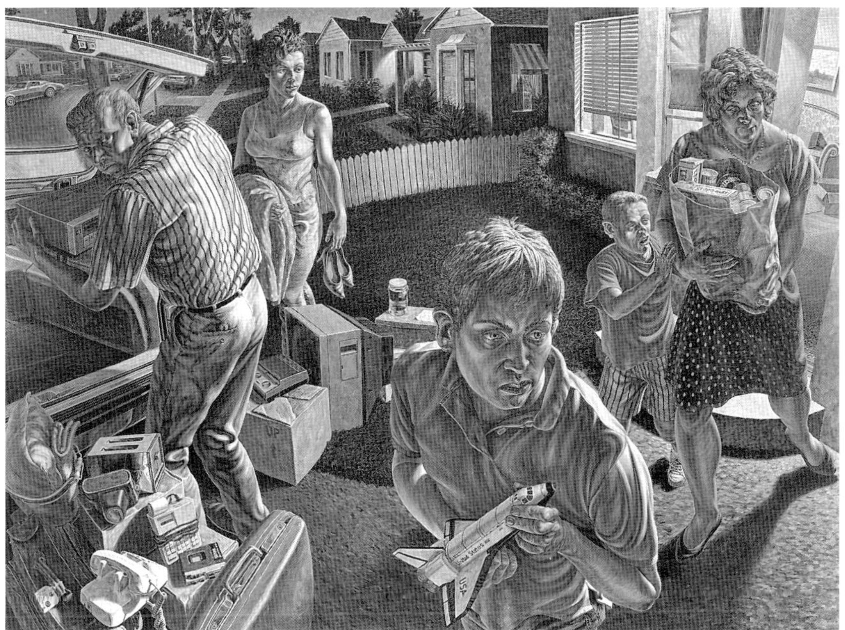

Midnight Exit, oil on canvas, 86 x 120". Courtesy Ovsey Gallery. Photo: Douglas M. Parker

F. Scott Hess was educated at the University of Wisconsin and the Vienna Academy of Fine Art. He has had a dozen solo exhibitions and participated in more than 35 group exhibitions since 1976. A recipient of the NEA, the J. Paul Getty and the WESTAF awards, and a winner of the Theodor Koerner and Rudolf Hausner prizes from Austria, F. Scott Hess is also represented in many public collections in the United States, Europe and the Near East.

Commissions considered.

Hess' work can be seen at Ovsey Gallery, Los Angeles, (213) 935-1883.

Studio visits by appointment: (213) 667-2921. His studio is located at 1830 Lake Shore Avenue, Los Angeles, CA 90026.

Shingo Honda

Painting

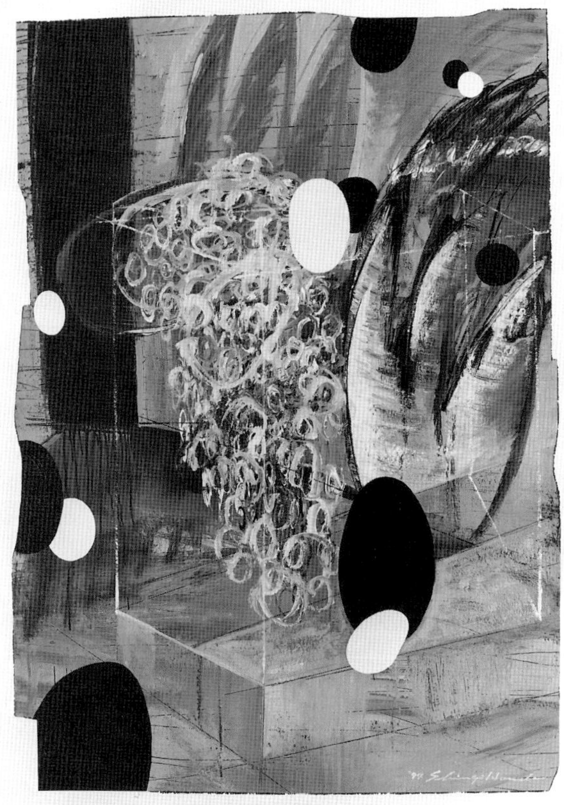

Case #47, acrylic on canvas, 63 x 47". Photo: Daniel Uppendahl

Shingo Honda's theme is change: constant change as the natural order of life within the harmonious whole.

He paints in oil and acrylic on canvas and on paper.

Honda's work is in corporate, private and museum collections. He is represented by: Atagoyama Gallery, Tokyo, (03) 357-5508, Lizardi/Harp Gallery, Pasadena, (818) 792-8336; Lois Neiter Fine Arts, Sherman Oaks, (818) 788-2158; and Art Resource Group, Laguna Beach, (714) 497-8282.

His work may also be purchased or rented from Art Rental and Sales Gallery, Los Angeles County Museum of Art, Los Angeles, (213) 857-6500, and Art Dimensions Inc., Santa Monica, (310) 828-5532.

Studio visits by appointment. For studio address and directions call (213) 626-3948.

Randall Lavender

Painting

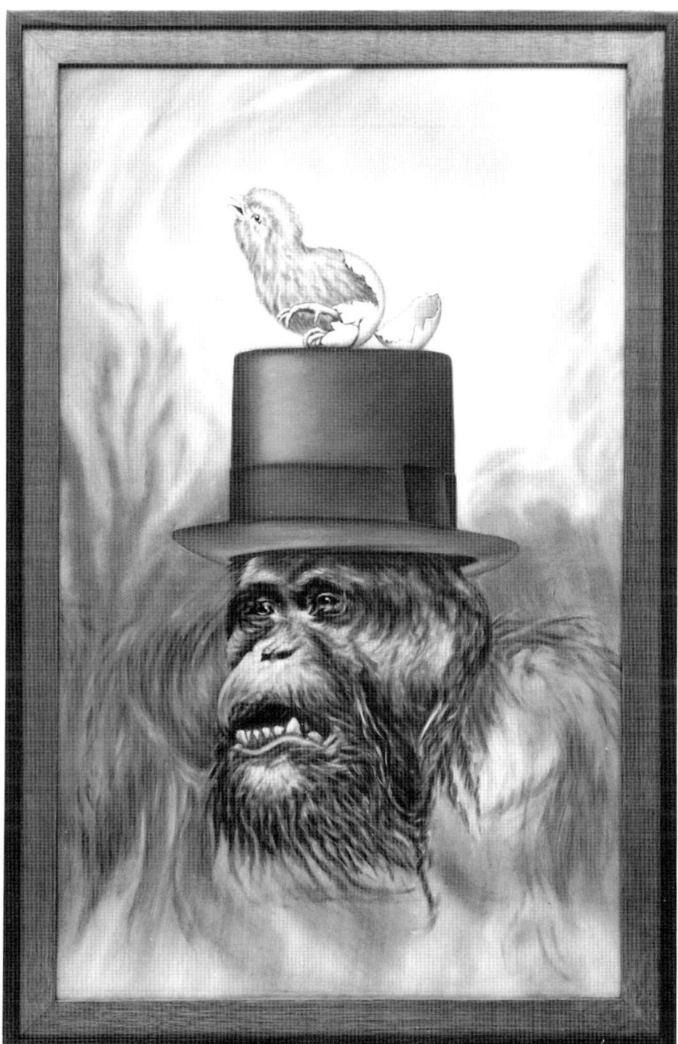

Day of Wonder, oil on panel, 34 x 22 1/2". Photo: Susan Einstein

Commissions accepted.

Lavender's work can be seen at Tortue Gallery, Santa Monica, (310) 828-8878.

Studio visits by appointment: (213) 589-7281. His studio is located at 2421 South Santa Fe Avenue, Studio 20, Los Angeles, CA 90058.

Gloria Longval

Painting

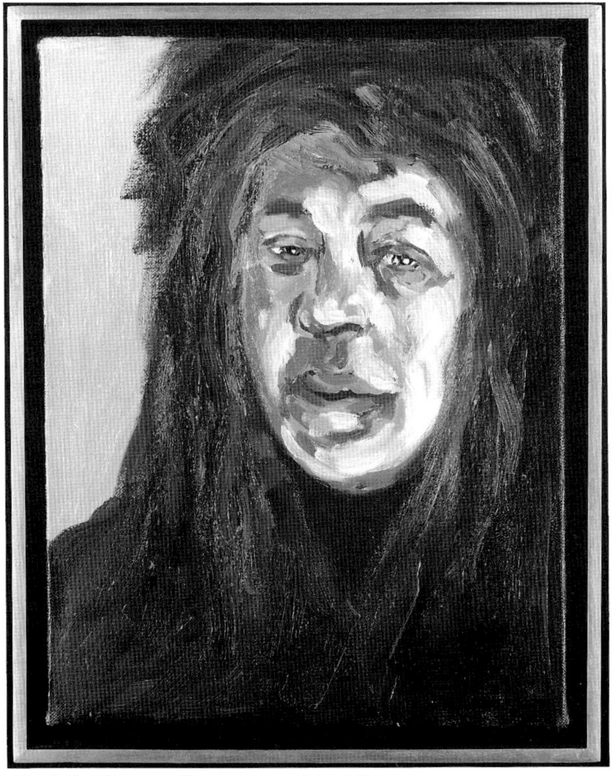

Head of a Woman, oil on canvas, 14 x 11"

Gloria Longval is a figurative painter. Her works are intimate, personal and narrative, dealing with the mystery, elusiveness and beauty of the human condition. She builds up her canvases with lush, thick layers of paint in rich hues and expressive textures, capturing an intense, mesmerizing quality.

Longval studied at the Art Student's League and the National Academy School of Fine Arts in New York City, having been awarded competitive scholarships. She exhibits widely in both solo and group exhibitions. Her works are in private and public collections in the United States, England, Mexico, Canada, Italy and Cuba. She is the recipient of numerous awards and has been extensively published.

Media: Oil and acrylic on canvas.

Studio visits by appointment: (213) 680-2858. Her studio is located at 201 South Santa Fe Avenue, #201, Los Angeles, CA 90012.

Gloria Moses

Painting

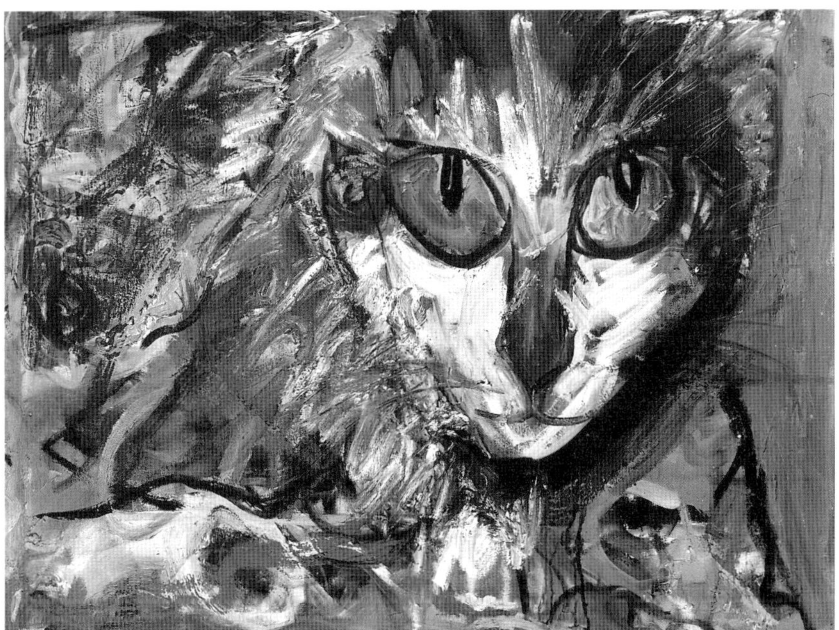

Wild Cat, oil on canvas, 40 x 30"

Gloria Moses paints large canvases of gardens, animals and landscapes in bold colors. The oil paintings reflect the tranquil view of nature that surrounds her airy, well lit studio. She also does figurative monoprints that show an edge of immediacy and exposed passion as well as ceramic sculptures with whimsical expressions. She moves from oils to watercolors to ceramics to printmaking and back again. Each seems to feed the others.

Moses is a signature member of the National Watercolor Society, Watercolor USA Honor Society and the National Printmaking Society.

Commissions accepted for ceramic animals and animal paintings.

Moses' work can be seen at Orlando Gallery, Sherman Oaks, (818) 789-6012; and Valerie Miller Fine Art, Palm Desert, (619) 773-4483.

Studio visits are by appointment: (310) 837-3738. Her studio is located at 2307 Bagley Avenue, Los Angeles, CA 90034.

Laurel Paley

Painting

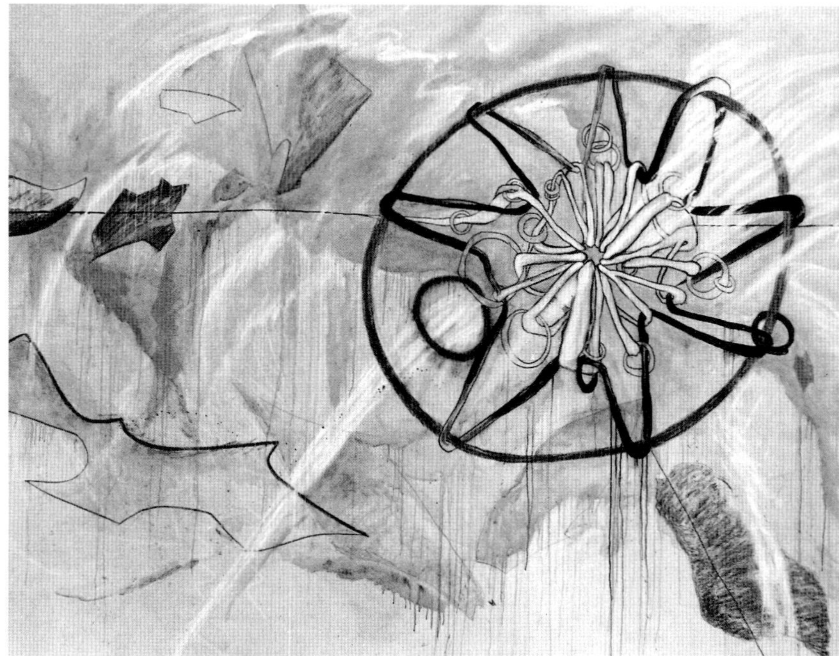

Links and Intervals: Web, oil and drawing media on canvas, 67 x 84"
Photo: Robert Wedemeyer

Laurel Paley's paintings are abstract visual narratives. Lines, marks, pictographs and images emerge from and fade into a wash of pale, dream-like colors, in a web of suggestions and juxtapositions. The work ranges in size, from intimately scaled etchings and drawings to bigger-than-life-sized work on canvas. Both open and autobiographical, the paintings, drawings and prints invite each viewer to interpret, question and discover.

Widely exhibited and reviewed, Laurel Paley's award-winning work can be found in numerous corporate and private collections. Paley also has taught drawing, printmaking and painting at area colleges, giving lectures and workshops to diverse groups, from museum docents, to prison inmates to at-risk teenagers.

Commissions accepted.

Paley's work can be seen at The Art Works, Riverside, (909) 781-6844.

Studio visits by appointment: (213) 587-0782.

Roland Reiss

Painting

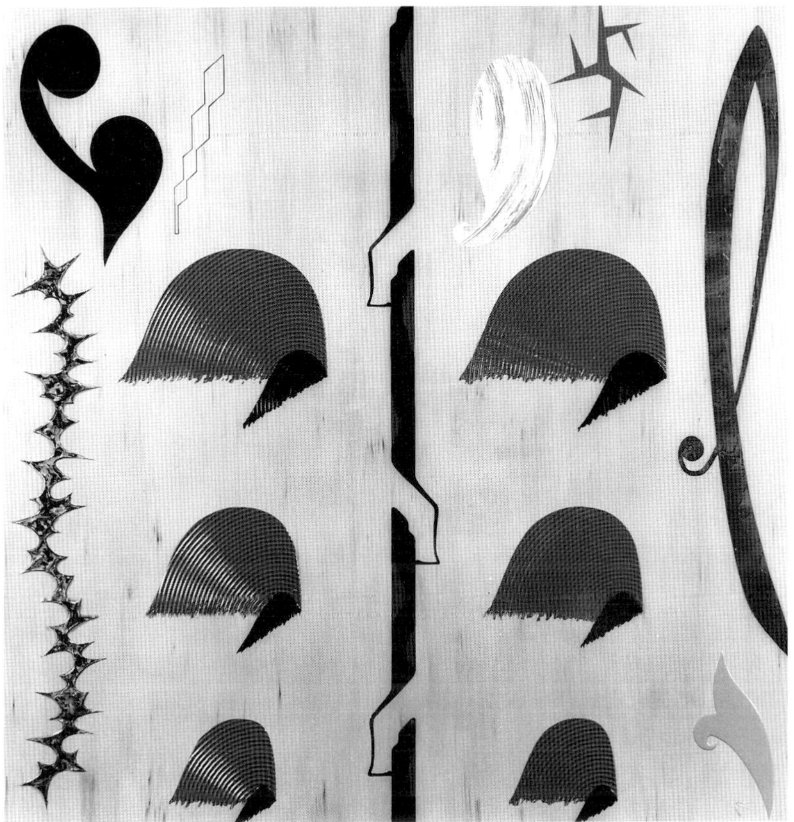

Red Rover, oil, acrylic and epoxy on panel, 7 x 7'

Roland Reiss has exhibited extensively in the United States and abroad. His work has been seen at the Whitney Museum of American Art and at *Documenta* in Kassel, Germany. Exhibitions include museums in Brazil, Mexico, Japan and Taiwan. He is the recipient of four NEA grants and of more than forty prizes and awards. His work is located in public, corporate, and private collections.

Since 1992, Reiss has concentrated exclusively on abstract painting. The paintings range in size from 8 x 8' to 2 x 2'.

Media: Oil, acrylic and epoxy on canvas and panel.

Prints and prices available on request.

Studio visits by appointment. Call for address and directions: (213) 221-9066.

Richard Sedivy

Painting

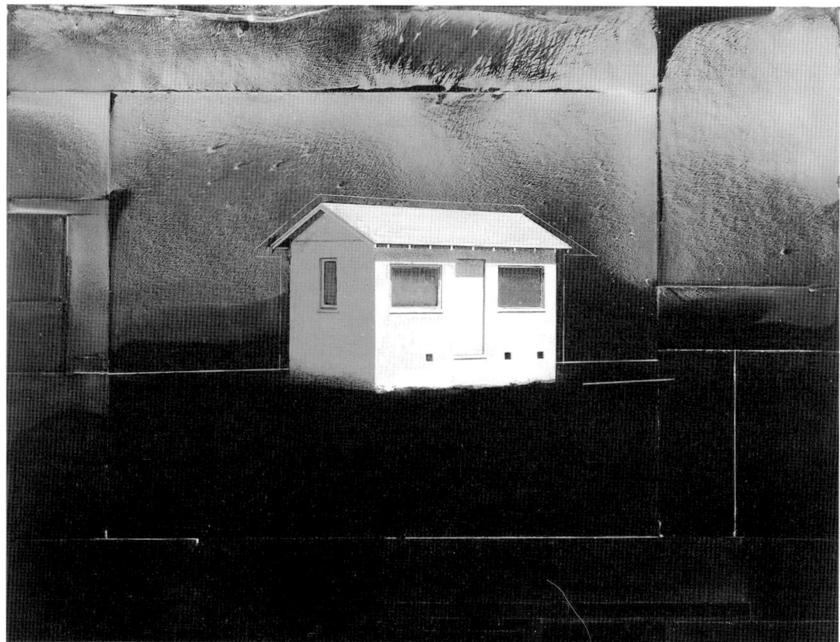

Pictorial America (American Dream), oil, varnish, screen ink on wood and masonite, 29 1/2 x 39"
Photo: Douglas M. Parker

Richard Sedivy has been a resident of Los Angeles for more than 20 years.

His work deals with the central issue of identity, and specifically self, as reflected in our surroundings, made metaphorical in images of architecture, dwelling and possessions, and delineated through the ideas of difference and similarity.

Sedivy's work varies in scale from small through large on a variety of wood and board materials, painted in a variety of oil and lacquer mediums.

Commissions accepted.

Studio visits by appointment: (213) 255-9186.

Norma Jean Squires

Painting

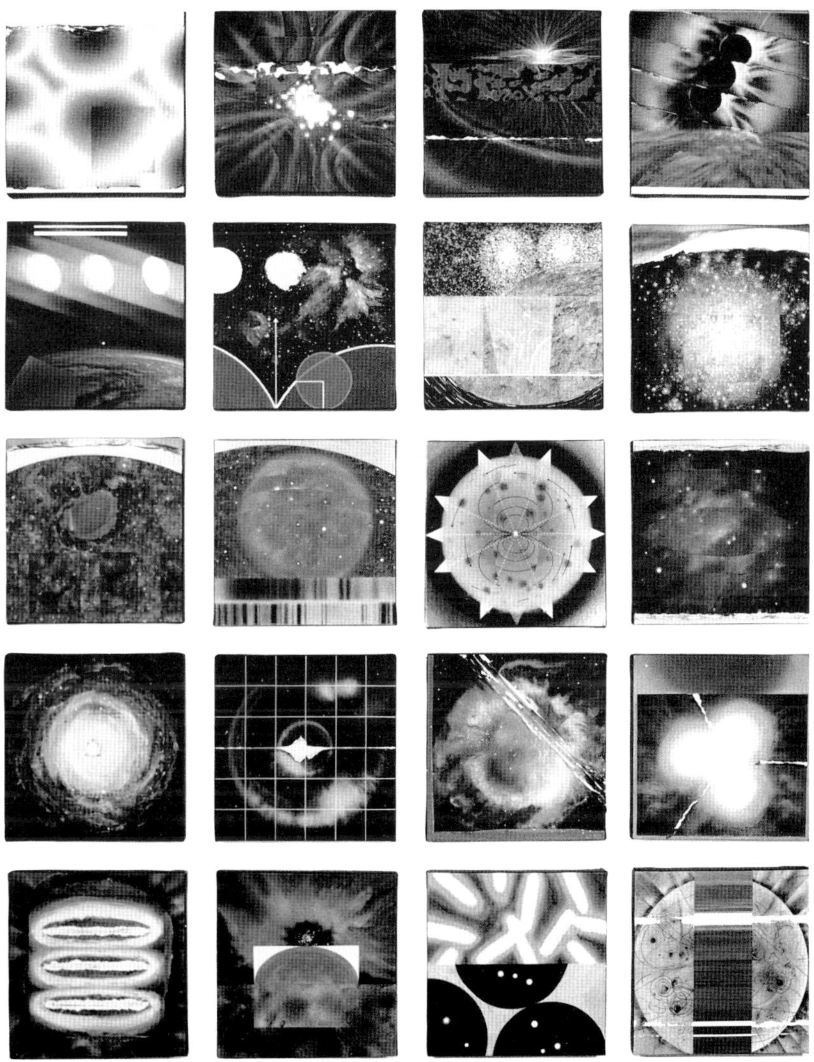

Read-out on a Sphere, acrylic on canvas. Photo: Norma Jean Squires

Read-out on a Sphere is a large-scale work comprised of 20 panels, 12 x 12" each. When installed vertically (as shown) the piece measures 68 x 54". It can also be exhibited horizontally or in other formats.

Studio visits by appointment: (310) 474-6364. Squires' studio is located at 2764 Woodwardia Drive, Los Angeles, CA 90077.

Ed Freeman

Photography

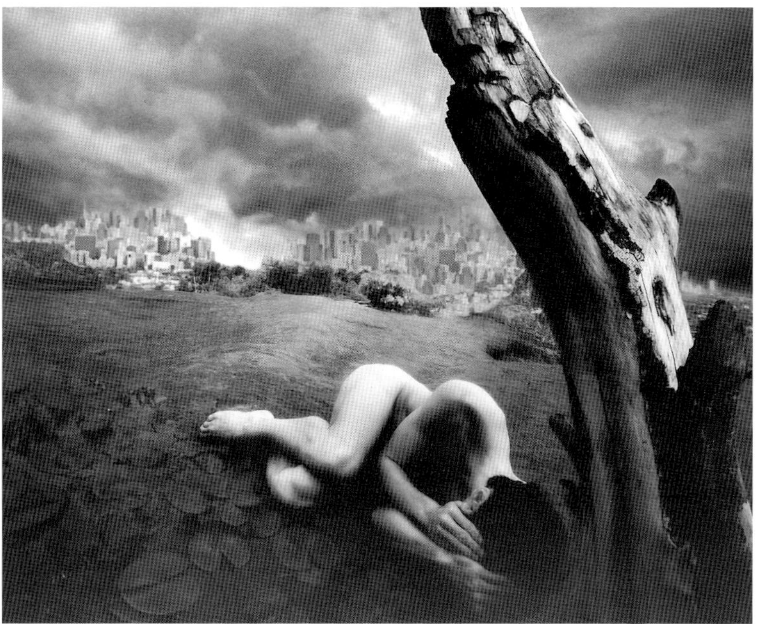

Dream City, black and white silver gelatin print, 11 x 14"

With the nude as his primary subject, Ed Freeman explores two widely divergent styles of photography: the classically crafted black and white print on the one hand, and on the other, heavily manipulated, impressionistic color work that looks like a cross between photography and rough pencil drawing, which in fact it is.

The black and white prints display a quiet emotion and meticulous control of lighting and composition; the color is more spontaneous, more voluptuous; both are celebrations more of form and spirit than of sexuality, and are restrained in their exploitation of nudity. Influences as diverse as Edward Weston, Robert Mapplethorpe and George Hurrell are evident.

Freeman's work has been widely exhibited in this country; his list of published works is extensive, both here and abroad. All works are printed in archival limited editions in a variety of sizes.

Commissions accepted. Prices available upon request.

To review the portfolio, call (213) 687-3113 for an appointment. Ed Freeman Photography is located at 912 East 3rd Street, #304, Los Angeles, CA 90013.

Richard Meade

Photography

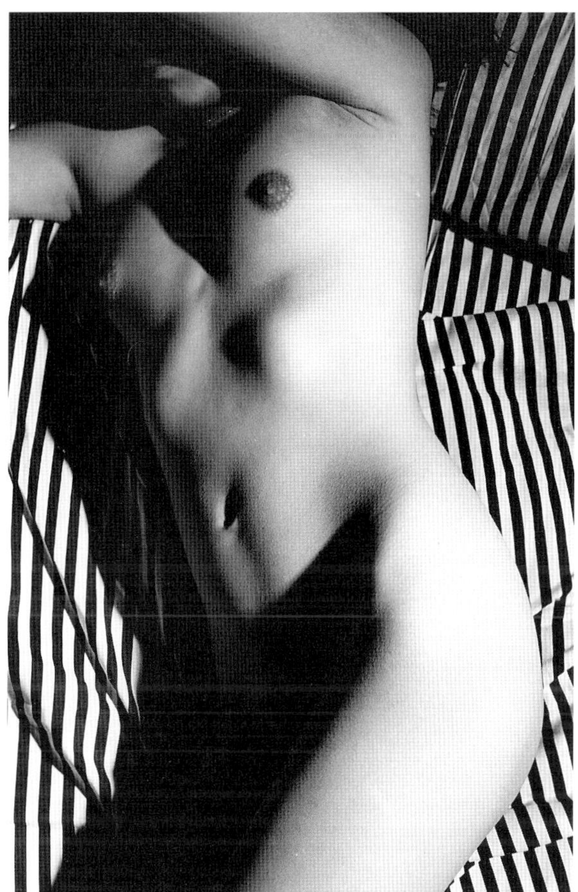

Illusory dislocation, black and white silver gelatin print, 12 3/4 x 19 1/4"

Richard Meade's work is a crossing point of technologies where contrasting lines meet: the rational and the intuitive, masculine and feminine, domestic and exotic, archetypal and private, ornamental and fundamental, digital and photosensitive.

Media: Black and white (silver gelatin), color (Cibachrome).

Meade's work can be seen at Granados 2 Gallery, Los Angeles, (213) 662-9930 and X-ibit Gallery, Los Angeles, (213) 380-1500.

Studio visits by appointment. Call for address and directions: (213) 662-6946.

Dora De Larios

Sculpture

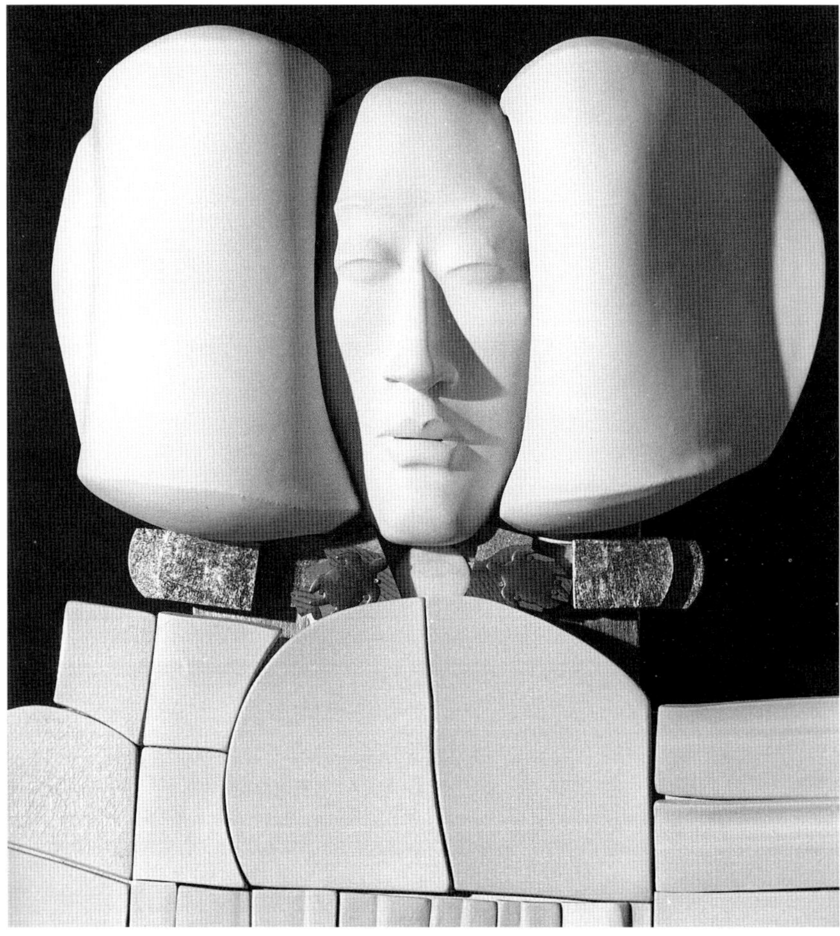

Goddess, stoneware, life size (detail). Photo: Chuck Bankutti

I am an artist -- first and foremost. I was given the gift to create and it has been my joy, strength, love and faith to do so in spite of the difficulties that have happened in my life. I have always produced good work and have been blessed in my life by having been surrounded by friends that have been supportive, spiritually and financially. My hope is to continue in good health to create until I drop. — Dora De Larios

Commissions accepted.

Studio visits by appointment: (310) 839-8305. De Larios' studio is located at 8560 Venice Boulevard, Los Angeles, CA 90034.

John F. Frame

Sculpture

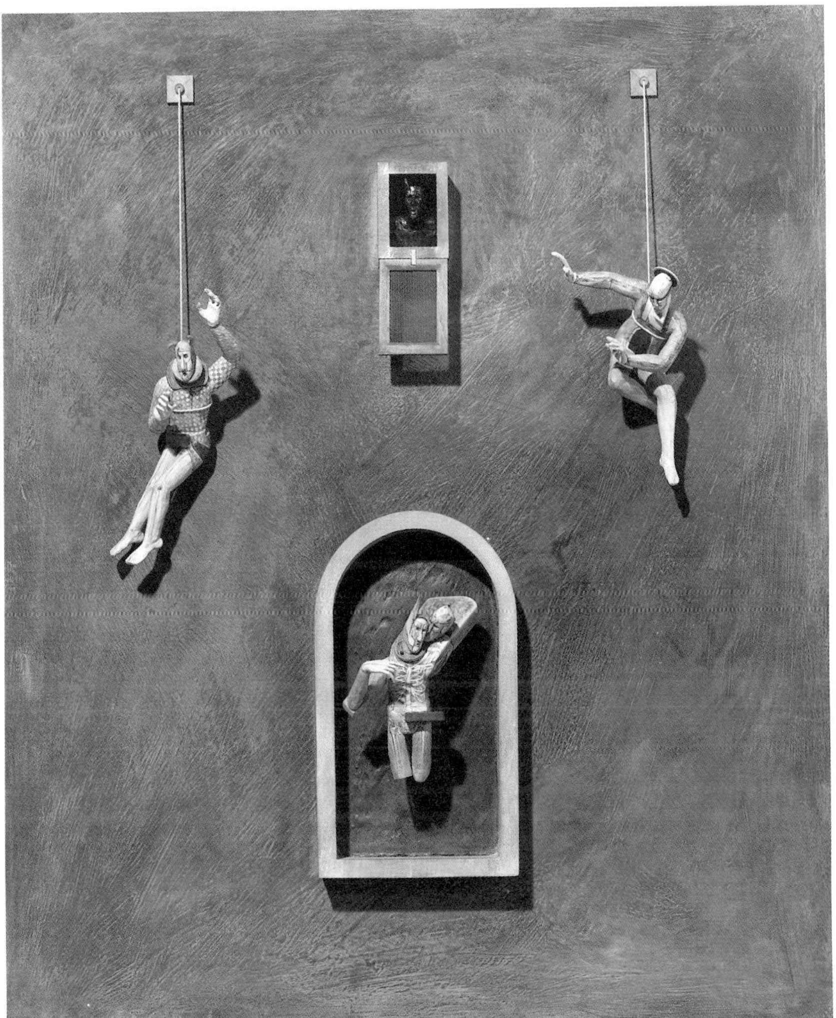

The Wick and the Wasp, 36 x 43 x 8", wood, bronze, brass, pigment, concrete
Photo: Douglas M. Parker

Commissions accepted.

Frame's work can be seen at Kohn Turner Gallery, Los Angeles, (310) 271-4453.

Studio visits by appointment: (213) 585-6593. Frame's studio is located at 2421 South Santa Fe Avenue, #21, Los Angeles, CA 90058.

Richard Gerrish

Sculpture

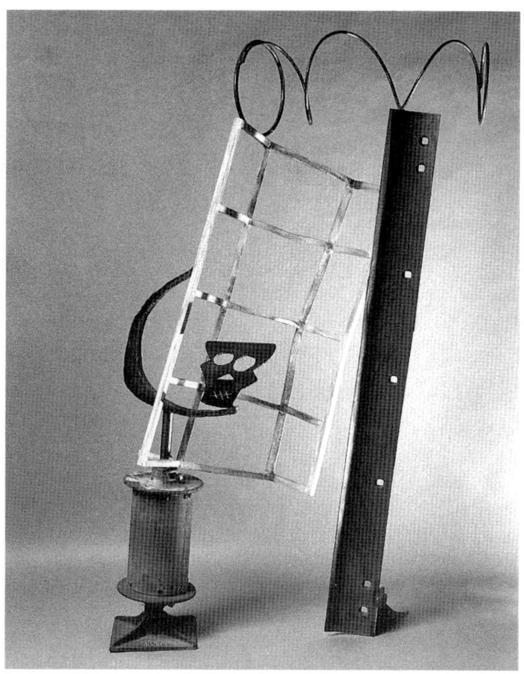

Blue Moon, polychromed welded steel, 70 x 45 x 15"

Richard Gerrish's artistic vision is to psychologically confront, philosophically stimulate, and ultimately delight his audience. He strives for an aesthetic balance between visual form and conceptual information, and he believes that simplicity of form and economy of imagery can most effectively project this message. Gerrish works in cut and welded polychromed steel.

Since graduating with an M.F.A. from Claremont Graduate School in 1980, he has shown world-wide in venues that include Finland, Japan, New York, Los Angeles and San Francisco. Gerrish currently serves on the board of directors of the Downtown Arts Development Association (DADA). He has been selected by the Community Redevelopment Agency to head a design team for the South Park Gateways Project in downtown Los Angeles.

Commissions accepted.

Gerrish's work can be seen at DADA, Los Angeles, (213) 629-5539.

Studio visits by appointment: (213) 587-5902. Gerrish Studio is located at 2349 South Santa Fe Avenue, Studio B, Los Angeles, CA 90058.

Maddy LeMel

Sculpture

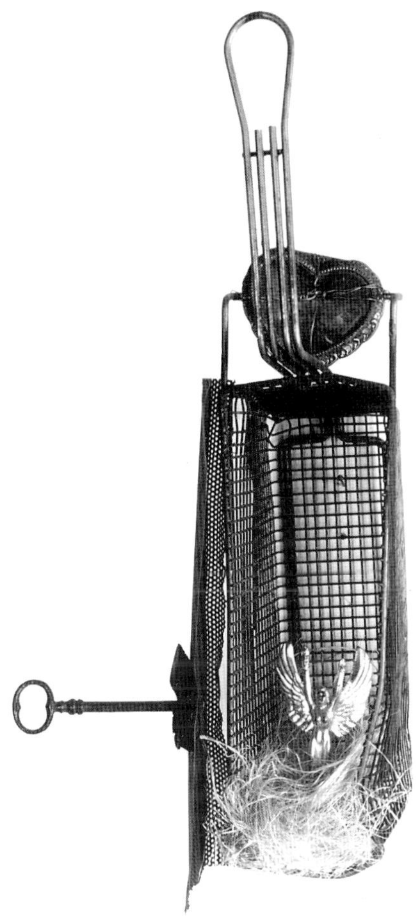

Untitled, mixed media, 20 1/2 x 5 x 9 1/2"

I am working with objects that have served their purpose as part of a larger whole. They have met their fate in a junkyard or discarded, are useless and decaying.

These objects are placed with others that they never would have happened upon in their original lifetime. The sculptures offer a reincarnation, giving rise to new life and meaning — a second chance.

— Maddy LeMel

Studio visits by appointment: (310) 476-9974.

Tanya Ragir

Sculpture

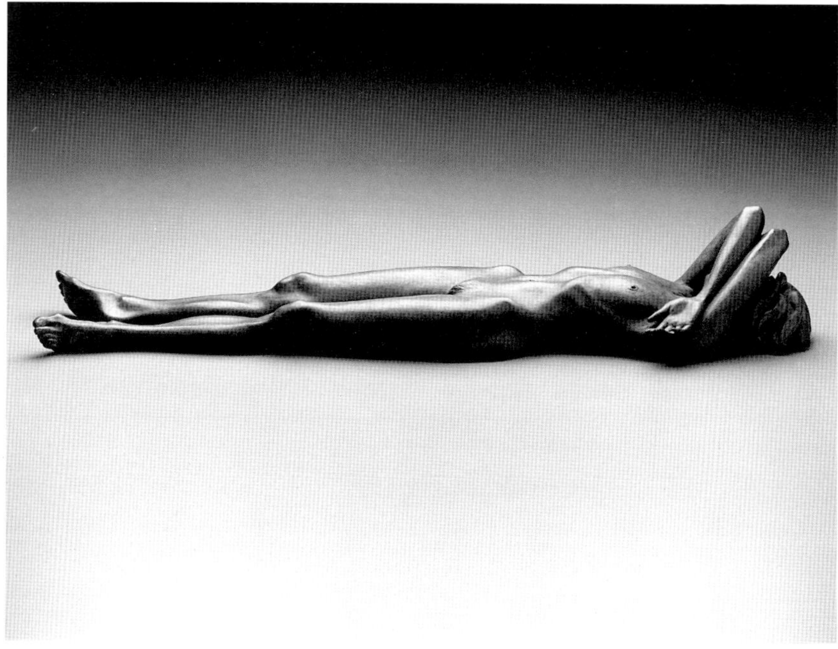

Intimacy, bronze (edition of 9), 36 x 6 x 5 1/2". Photo: Ron Krisel

For many years, California-born artist Tanya Ragir has worked classically with the female form, sculpting in clay and casting in resin or bronze. Recently, she has been drawn to looking at the figure through geometric "windows," isolating details and altering the scale. This allows her to be at once more intimate with and have more separation from the humanness of the form.

Ragir relates to human form as landscape and sees the relationship between all organic forms . . . "The way an interior fold or a ridge reminds me of the inside of a flower or the formation of a sand dune." She feels "very attracted to both the geometry and industrial nature of material, juxtaposed with sensual forms."

In a number of her sculptures there is a random arrangement of forms "which can be related to each other as parts of a quilt rather than as sections of the human body."

Commissions accepted.

Studio visits by appointment: (310) 398-6004. Ragir's studio is located at 3587 Ocean View Avenue, Los Angeles, CA 90068.

Bob Stimmel

Sculpture

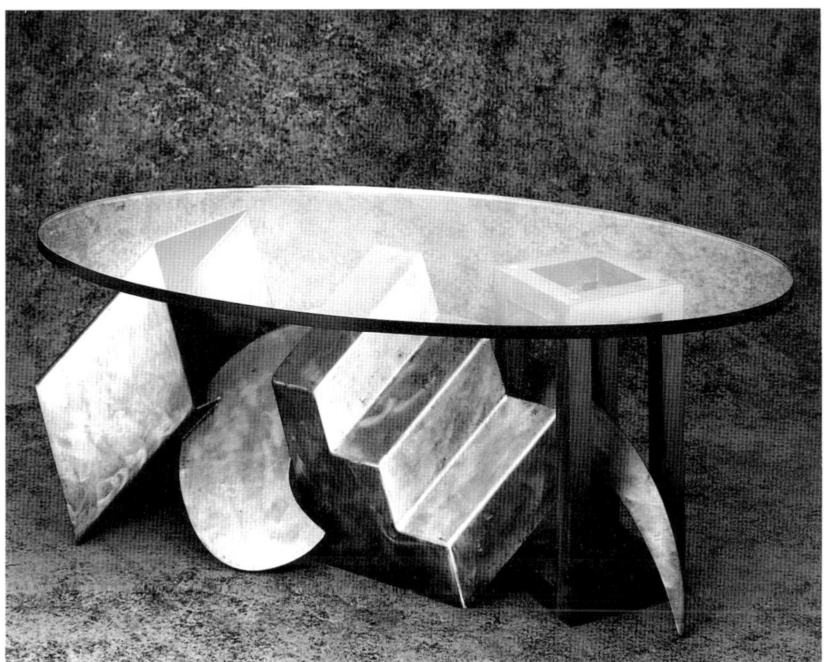

Steelhenge Table, steel and glass, 18 x 48 x 27"

I approach making sculpture intuitively. A certain form or shape implies an emotion, and the emotion's need to express itself creates a visual story. By juxtaposing forms of painted and natural woods, steel, aluminum and bronze, I weave an abstract dialogue between myself and those who encounter my work. This desire for nonliteral expression is as ancient as the cave paintings and as timeless as the creative force itself.
— Bob Stimmel

Commissions accepted.

Stimmel's work can be seen at Nemiroff Deutsch Fine Art, Santa Monica (310) 315-5400; Valerie Miller Fine Art, Palm Desert, (619) 773-4483; and Karen Goodman Associates, Chicago, IL, (312) 482-9540.

Studio visits by appointment: (213) 469-5264. His studio is located at 2234 North Gower Street, Los Angeles, CA 90068.

Laurie Pincus

Mixed Media

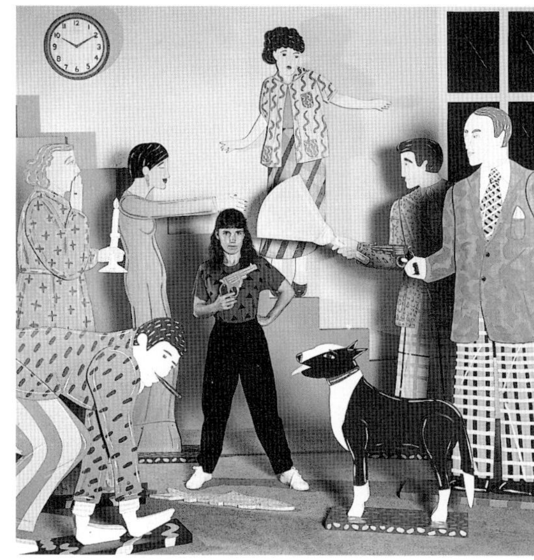

10:10
painted wood installation
life size
Photo: Marva Marrow
from *Inside the L.A. Artist*

My work is primarily about the imagination and visual storytelling. I work with paint, paper, wood, and canvas, in small scale and lifesize. The viewer is very important to me and to the continued unfolding of the story. I like to encourage the viewer literally to enter the visual story and become one of the figures/characters there, letting my art become a bridge that connects fantasy with reality. — Laurie Pincus

Laurie Pincus has never gotten out of touch with her childhood; her paintings and sculptures are part of a direct continuum that began when, as an infant, she separated her crayons into male and female characters and made up stories about them. Today, her characters range from hand-held to life size, but they are still crayon-bright in color, and they still move through worlds generated by Pincus' imagination. These worlds are fantastic but they are also based on reality. They have the naiveté of a child's vision, but the haunting truth of social commentary. — Betty Ann Brown, *Artweek*

Laurie Pincus began exhibiting her work in 1979, having had more than 70 shows in the United States and Japan, including a ten-year retrospective at Loyola Marymount University in Los Angeles in 1989-90. Her work is represented in many corporate and private collections.

Commissions accepted.

Visits to her studio, Imagination Workshop, are by appointment: (310) 459-4520.

Gary McCloy

Ceramic Vessels

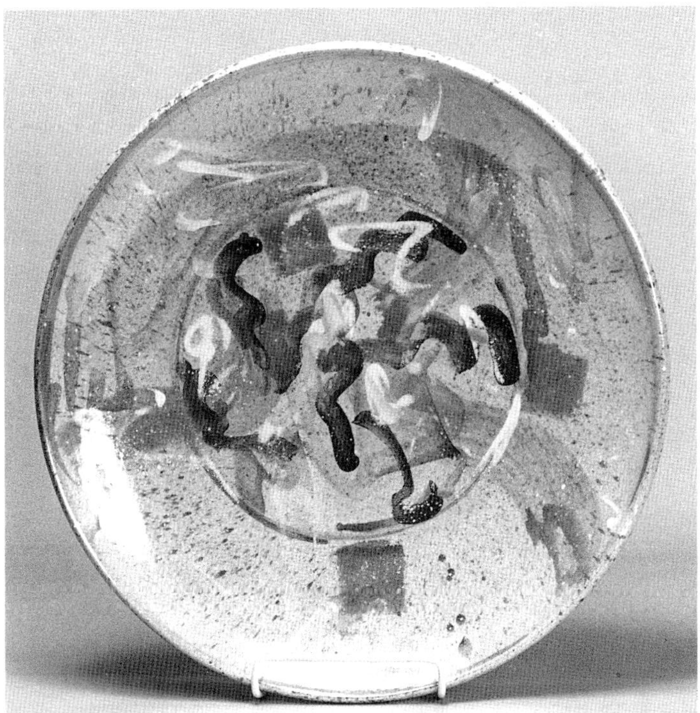

Decorated plate, wheel thrown, 26" diameter x 4" high. Photo: Gary McCloy

Gary McCloy has been making one-of-a-kind ceramic vessels for 25 years. His work with wheel-thrown and hand-built clay is well known for its richly glazed surfaces. Each piece may undergo as many as 15 firings to build a lustrous surface of color and design.

McCloy specializes in custom vessels for residential and commercial interiors. His work has been shown in *Architectural Digest, Interior Design, Metropolitan Home* and Los Angeles magazines.

Recent commissions include vessels for major installations in London, Singapore, Tokyo, Hong Kong, Sydney, Honolulu, Guam, Saudi Arabia, San Francisco, Tucson and Chicago.

Commissions accepted.

His work can be seen at Initials, Los Angeles, (213) 653-6300; Blake House, Laguna Niguel, (714) 831-8292; and Burke-Tiller Studio, Rancho Mirage, (619) 770-6000.

Studio visits by appointment: (619) 322-6430.

Philipp Scholz Rittermann

Photography

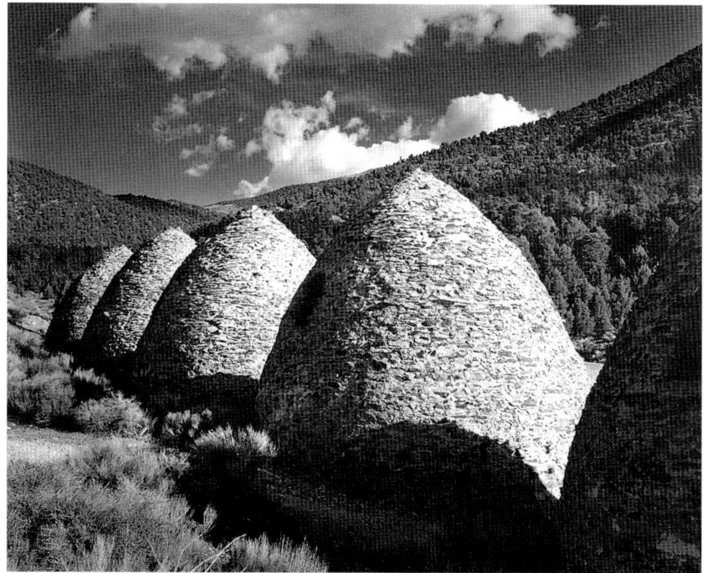

Charcoal Kilns, Death Valley, California, black and white silver gelatin print
12 x 16" to 40 x 50"

Philipp Scholz Rittermann began his artistic career in 1977. His images act as catalysts, raising questions rather than answering them. He strives to create work that is both compelling and ambiguous. He seeks to tap each viewer's sense of discovery.

After a decade of photographing the urban world at night, he began photographing landscape, encompassing both healthy and poisoned places. The tenor of this work fluctuates from serene to ominous, less a manifesto than a personal chronicle. At times, he combines large prints, creating relationships between two or more images.

Featured in more than 60 solo and group exhibitions in the U.S., Europe, Canada and Mexico, his photographs grace public and private collections from the Museum of Modern Art in New York to the Bibliotheque Nationale in Paris.

Commissions accepted.

Scholz Rittermann's work can be seen at David Zapf Gallery, San Diego, (619) 232-5004; Paul Kopeikin Gallery, Los Angeles, (213) 937-0765; and Benteler-Morgan Galleries, Houston, TX, (713) 522-8228.

Visits to Philipp Scholz Rittermann Photography are by appointment: (619) 297-7838.

Jeffery Laudenslager

Sculpture

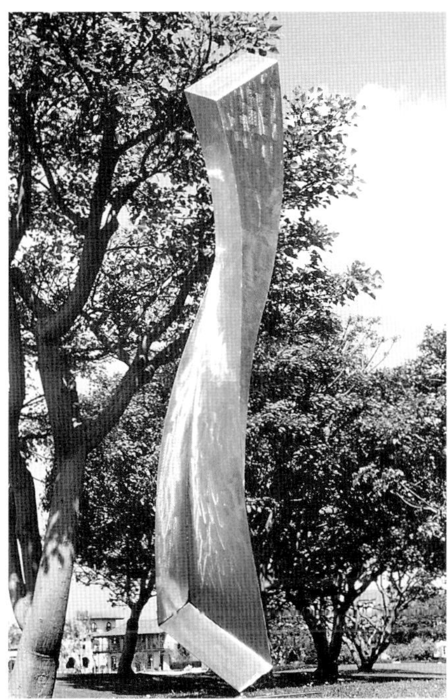

Deanna, steel
8 1/2 x 2 x 2'

My work has often been referred to as illusionist, and to a degree that is valid. A more accurate adjective is . . . elusive. I make objects that "appear" to be familiar, but they are ambiguous representations of what we "know" to be real. For example, *Circle* is an ideal form, a concept, which we seldom experience in reality. What we generally experience in the world are elliptical shapes of various proportions which we "see" as circles. I reverse this situation in my sculpture. I provide the experience of a circle by creating an ellipse in reality. By reversing the roles of reality and perception, tension is created between what is seen and what is believed.

A psychiatrist, who collects my work, refers to viewing the objects as "working the brain." — Jeffery Laudenslager

Commissions accepted.

Laudenslager's work can be seen at SOMA Gallery, San Diego, (619) 232-3955; Carl Schlosberg Fine Art, Sherman Oaks, (818) 783-6209; and Harcourts Contemporary, San Francisco, (415) 421-3428.

Studio visits by appointment: (619) 544-0133. His studio is located at 1041 J Avenue, San Diego CA 92101.

Deanne Sabeck

Sculpture / Architectural Embellishment

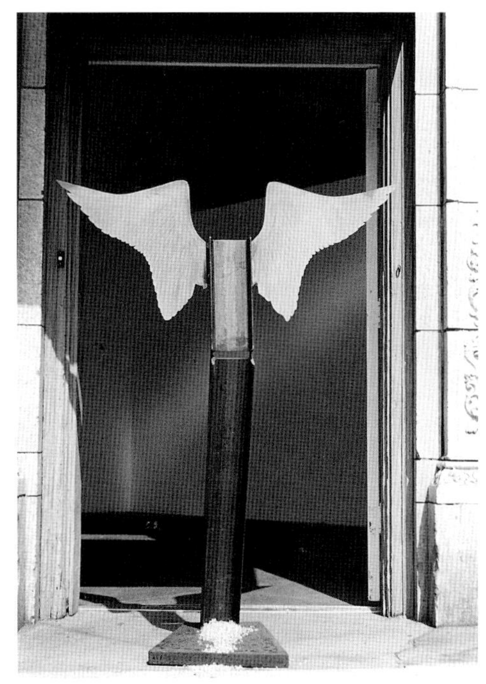

Metamorphosis
glass, steel, fabric and
projected light, 5 1/2 x 4 x 4'

Coming from a background of embellishing architectural spaces with color and light, my current work moves beyond my architectural background into a more personal realm. Using projected light, words and symbols, I create illusive messages that provoke intimate thought and emotion. Translucent glass wings elevating a steel I-beam, a transformation in process. A winged altarpiece with projected words and shadows moving fluidly on the wall.

The materials I use are crucial as they represent the complex contradictions in life: fragility/strength, lightness/heaviness, transparency/opacity, fluidity/solidity. These complex relationships of contradiction intrigue me, and it is my intent as an artist to share this experience with others. — Deanne Sabeck

Commissions accepted.

Sabeck's work can be seen at Patricia Correia Gallery, Venice, (310) 314-2626; and Kuivato Glass Studio and Gallery, Sedona AZ, (602) 282-1212.

Studio visits by appointment: (619) 234-0814. Sabeck's studio is located at 710 13th Street, #215, San Diego, CA 92101.

William Michael Schindler

Sculpture

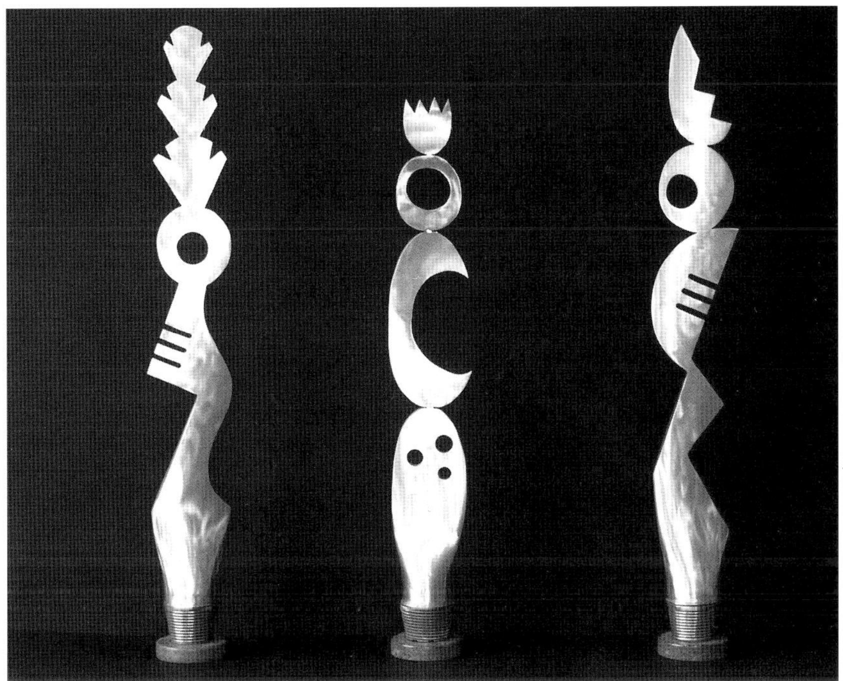

Iacocca, Tulip Queen, Mandolin, aluminum on marble base, left to right, 45 x 5" diam., 36 x 5", 41 x 5"

William Michael Schindler's sculptures transform industrial castoffs into objects of aesthetic value and beauty. He has constructed dynamic wall sculptures from marble fragments, granite cut-offs, machined aluminum and acid-washed copper. He has shaped graceful table sculptures out of brass rudders from navy ships. He has also created intricate, free-standing floor sculptures from blue, anodized aluminum tubes.

His work is testimony to the transforming power of art over even discarded materials, and a metaphor for what Schindler believes is the transforming power of ideas on human lives.

Commissions accepted.

Schindler's studio is located at 903 K Street, San Diego, CA 92101. Hours are Monday through Friday, 1-5pm, or by appointment: (619) 584-2314.

Ciel Bergman aka Cheryl Bowers

Painting

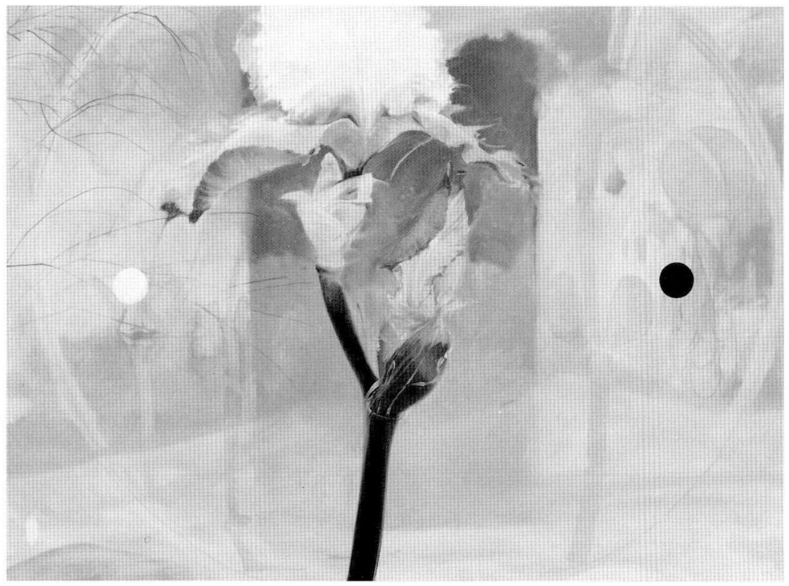

A Single Flower Can Last in the Ocean Forever, oil, wax and alkyd, 5 x 7"
Photo: William Dewey

These are paintings of hope, celebrating the world's beauty while confronting its darkness. There are wounds here, laid bare so that they might be healed, but there is also peace, resolution. . . . — Ben Marks, *ArtWeek*

We desperately need a transforming vision, one in which hope, beauty, optimism, courage, collaboration, relatedness and imagination — the best qualities of which we are capable — are honored. My work takes a path between reality and nonreality, disparate perceptions cohering in the simultaneous instant.

I search to unearth the Deep Feminine, which has not had voice for over 3,000 years. I revere the natural world. We suffer a taboo against beauty as a value in our culture. I feel the recovery of beauty is essential to our survival. The soul thrives on beauty. The creation of art is, I believe, a spiritual practice. — Ciel Bergman

Commissions accepted.

Bergman's work can be seen at Ro Snell Gallery, Santa Barbara, (805) 966-0903 and Laura Carpenter Gallery, Santa Fe, NM, (505) 986-9090.

She is currently working in New Mexico. Studio visits by appointment: (505) 638-5392. Her mailing address is P. O. Box 95, Coyote, NM 87012.

Ali Gobelle

Painting

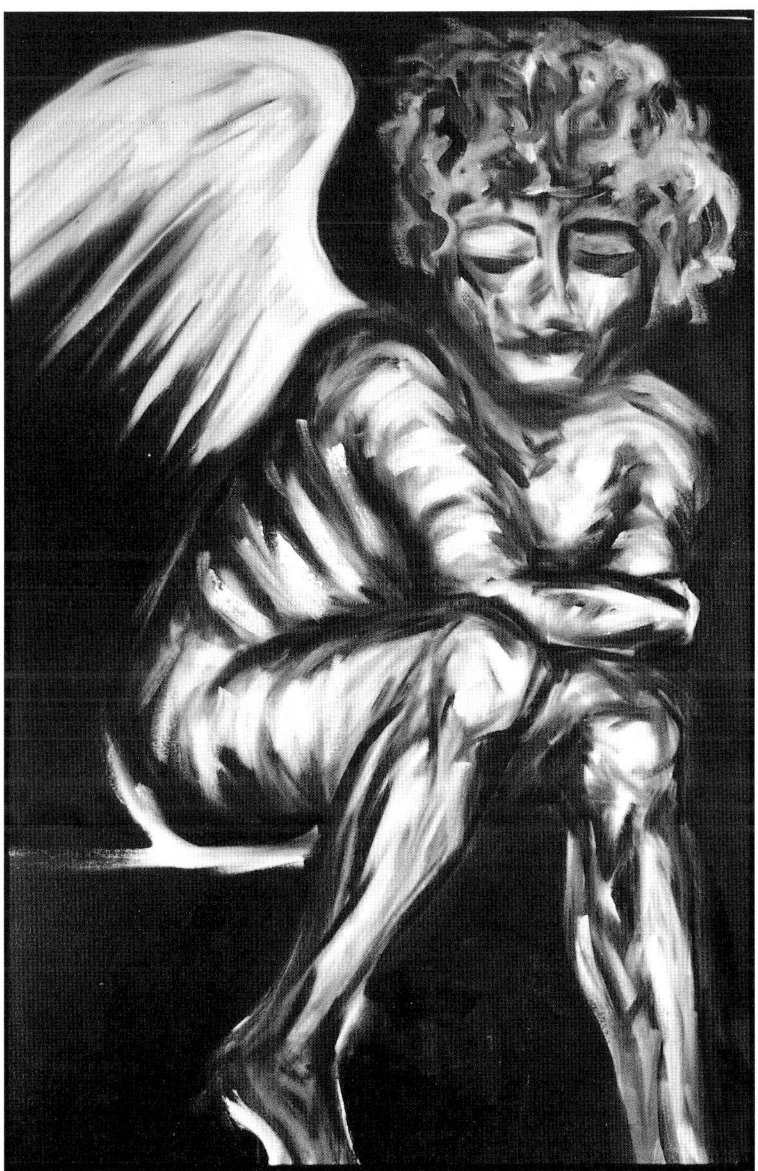

The Angel of Regret, oil on canvas, 34 x 48"

Studio visits by appointment: (805) 963-4158.

Jane Gottlieb

Mixed Media

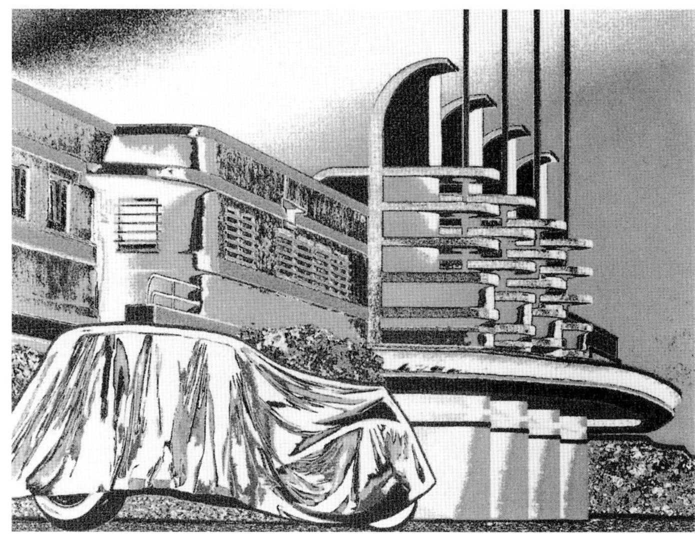

Draped Bentley, mixed media, 27 x 38"

Jane Gottlieb, an internationally exhibited artist, is a great believer in color as an invigorating life force. Gottlieb creates vibrant, dream-like images of such cultural icons as classic automobiles, art deco architecture and ancient monuments, using two distinct styles. The artist's earlier works were designed with her own technique in which she hand-painted Cibachrome prints with archival retouching dye. Gottlieb's newer works use cutting-edge computer technology to manipulate, combine, collage, paint and saturate her imagery.

Gottlieb's fine art images have been collected and exhibited in museums and galleries throughout the United States and Europe, including major shows in Los Angeles, Denver, New York, Rome and Milan.

Gottlieb's images challenge the viewer's vision by enhancing color, light and perspective to alter reality and stimulate new perceptions. The intent is to inspire a wide spectrum of emotion by utilizing contradiction, mystery and vivid, sensual color. "I try to lend a sense of hope and magic to the realities of modern life," relates Gottlieb.

Gottlieb's art work will be featured in a yearlong inaugural exhibition, *Joy Rides*, beginning in June 1994 at the new Los Angeles County Petersen Automotive Museum.

Commissions accepted.

Studio visits by appointment: (310) 573-1515.

Nancy Kay

Painting

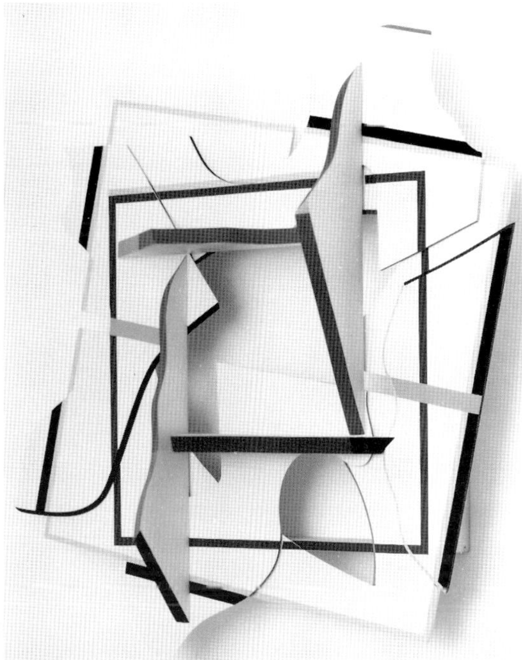

3-D Red Square, acrylic on polyvinyl, 27 x 27 x 10"
Photo: Brian Forrest

Nancy Kay is a futurist and contructivist. Her paintings and constructions consist of layered planes that contain intricately cut shapes and patterns. These forms are contradicted by the application of a single overall color or bright multi-colored fractured strips that activate the surface. The resulting compositions are both flat and dimensional. They appear static and dynamic and stand as both autonomous works and components of larger forms.

Kay's work has been featured in many gallery and museum shows nationally and internationally, including solo shows at Galerie Suzanne Bollag, Zurich, Switzerland and the Santa Monica Heritage Museum. Her work was part of that museum's traveling group exhibition *Prints by Los Angeles Artists*. She is included in numerous private and corporate collections.

Commissions accepted.

Studio visits by appointment. To see Kay's work call Sharon Truax Fine Art, Venice: (310) 396-3162.

Jim Morphesis

Painting

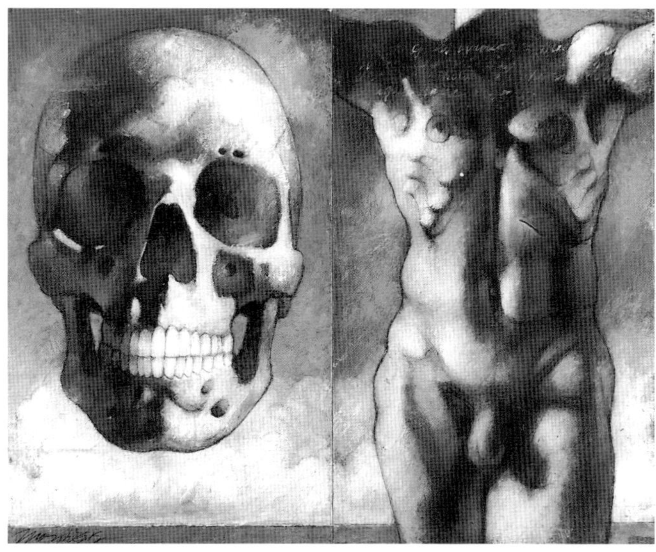

Revelations Series, No. 6, oil and graphite on wood panels, 16 x 20"
Photo: Kevin Noble

Recent Solo Exhibitions: 1994, Littlejohn/Sternau Gallery, New York, NY; 1994, Tortue Gallery, Santa Monica; 1993, The Works Gallery, Costa Mesa; 1993, Deson/Saunders Gallery, Chicago, IL.

Recent Group Exhibitions: 1994,*The Figure,* Shidoni Galleries, Santa Fe, NM; 1994-93, *Sanctuaries: Recovering the Holy in Contemporary Art,* The Museum of Contemporary Religious Art, St. Louis, MO; 1992, *Cruciformed: Images of the Cross Since 1980,* Cleveland Center for Contemporary Art, Cleveland, OH.

Awards: Louis Comfort Tiffany Foundation Biennial Award for Painting, Los Angeles County Museum of Art, Modern and Contemporary Art Council, Young Talent Purchase Award.

Selected Museum Collections: Laguna Art Museum, Los Angeles County Museum of Art, Metropolitan Museum of Art, The Oakland Museum, San Francisco Museum of Modern Art.

Commissions accepted.

Morphesis' work can be seen at Tortue Gallery, Santa Monica, (310) 828-8878.

He is currently working in New York City. Studio visits by appointment: (212) 334- 4835. His studio is located at 79 Leonard Street, B-1, New York, NY, 10013.

Jon Swihart

Painting

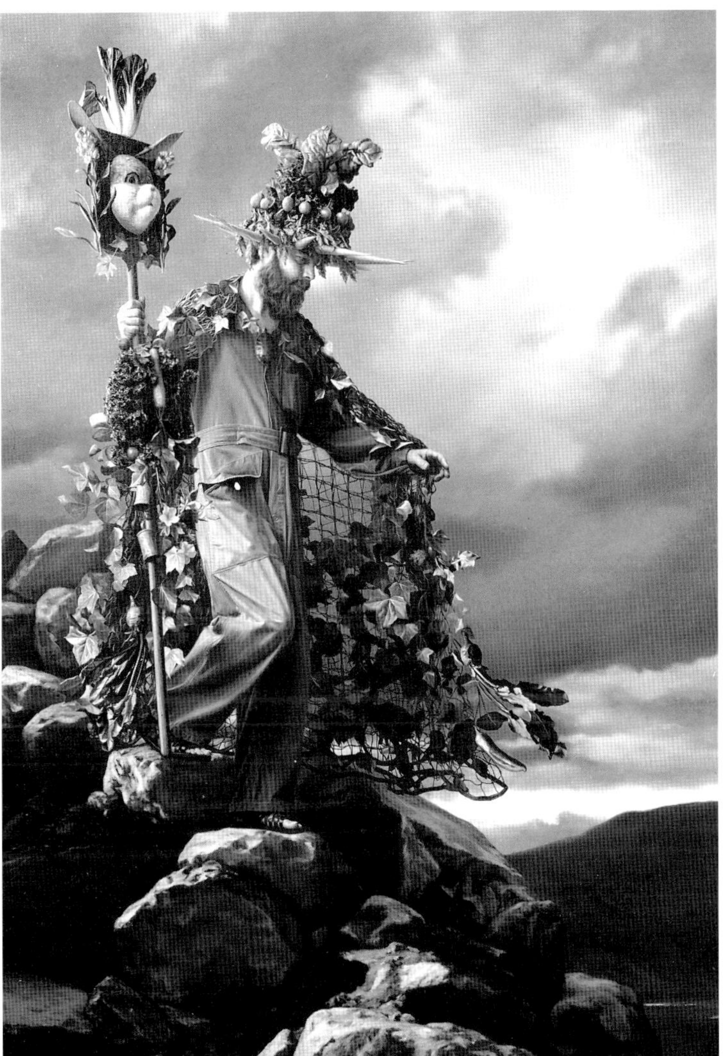

Untitled, oil on canvas, 36 x 26". Photo: Gene Ogami

Commissions accepted.

Swihart's work can be seen at Tortue Gallery, Santa Monica, (310) 828-8878.

Studio visits by appointment: (310) 452-3670. His studio is located at 1311 Pearl Street, Santa Monica, CA 90405.

Zevi Blum

Prints

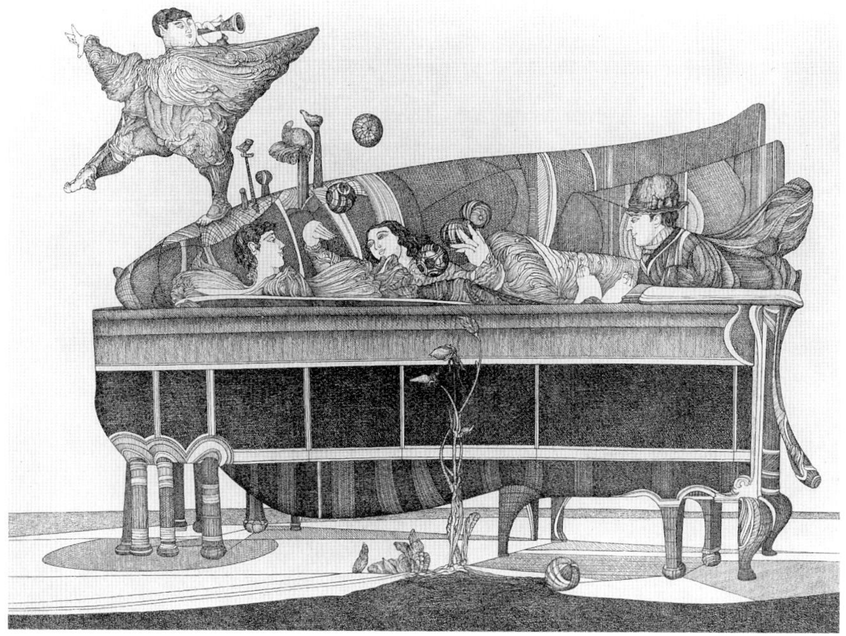

Hot Tub of Life, etching, 18 x 24". Photo: Emil Ghinger

I received by Bachelor of Architecture from Cornell University in 1957 and my New York State License several years later, after toiling in the architectural vineyard for a biblical seven years, I was offered a show at the Contemporaries Gallery in New York City. To my surprise and sadness, I never again returned to architecture on any basis.

Architecture represented my world of abstract relationship and art my personal subjective one. My work is in the tradition of Swift and Hogarth. My admiration is in the tradition of Oscar Wilde. My filter is architecture. — Zevi Blum

Blum's work can be seen at Parnas Gallery, Santa Monica (310) 458-6335.

He is currently working in Ithaca, New York. Studio visits by appointment: (607) 273-0088. His studio is located at 403 Mitchell Street, Ithaca, New York 14850.

Vanessa Obten

Sculpture

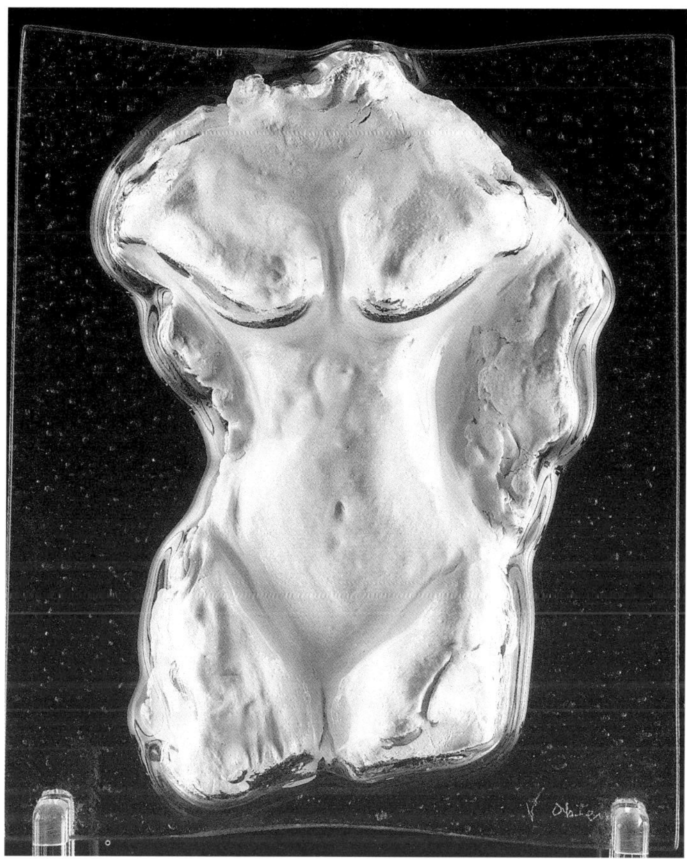

Untitled (bas relief), porcelain and glass, 12 x 14"

My dad is a sculptor and painter and while I was growing up, I spent a lot of time working with him. I can't remember a time when I wasn't intrigued with the process of creating things. The first time I worked with clay I knew that it was the material I would use. My current work combines porcelain and glass. The extremes embodied in these materials are, for me, a metaphor for the human condition. — Vanessa Obten

Obten's formal training included study at the Art Students League and the School of Visual Arts, both in New York City. Her work has been widely shown and collected.

Medium: Porcelain, glass and acrylic paint.

Studio visits by appointment: (310) 399-5245.

Jean Wolff

Sculpture

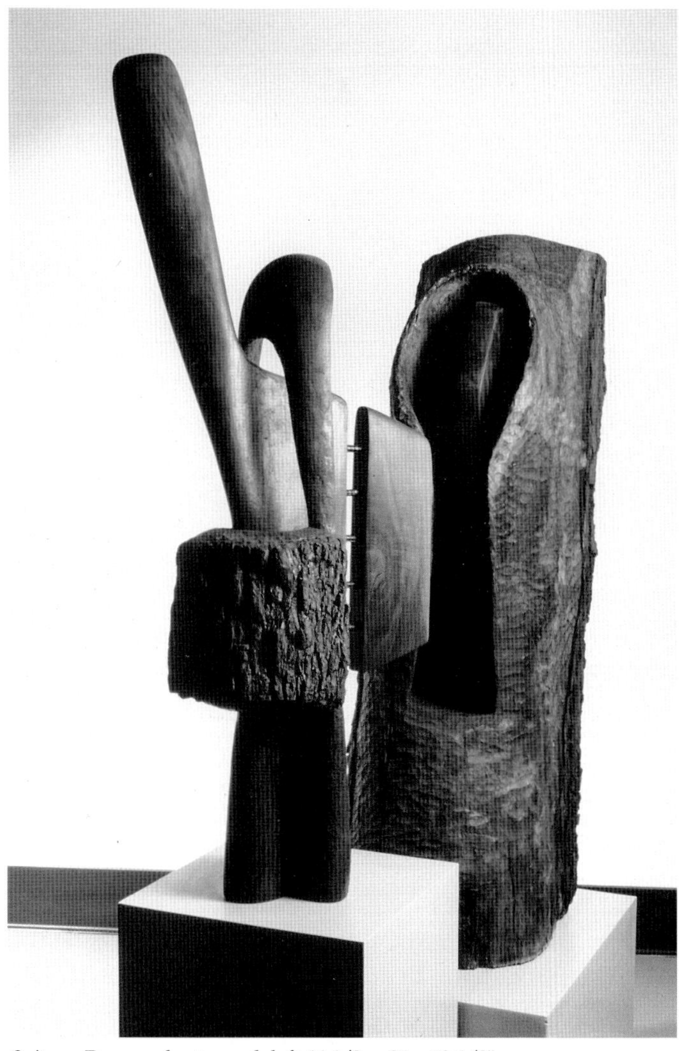

Suite en Deux, walnut wood, left 44 1/2 x 21 x 12 1/2",
right 43 1/2 x 16 1/2 x 9". Photo: Roger Marshutz

Media: Wood, bronze, stainless steel

Commissions accepted. Catalog and prices available upon request.

Wolff's work can be seen at La Quinta Sculpture Park, La Quinta, (619) 564-6464.

Studio visits by appointment: (310) 450-5831.

Jamy Kahn

Painting

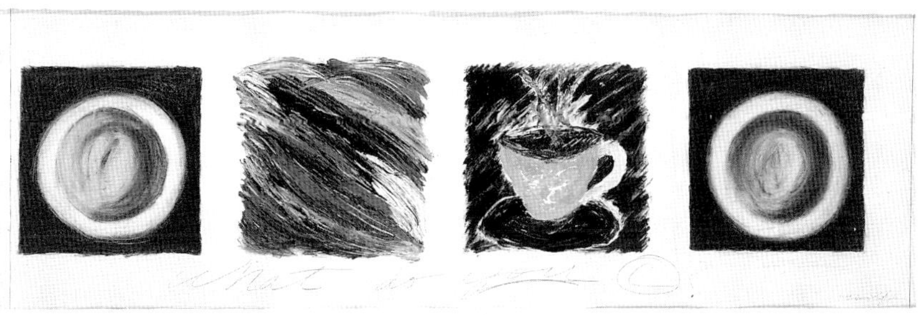

C-Quence, acrylic and pastel on paper, 84 x 26"

I am interested in those cultural institutions and habitual practices which provide the illusion of making us feel as if we have more *control* over our immediate universe and our lives. I often use coffee cups and teacups, teapots and other vessels because to me they represent the institution of the neighborhood coffee shop, the international ritual of tea time and meal time, or that sanctioned space in which we allow ourselves to sit down and connect to ourselves and others. — Jamy Kahn

Jamy Kahn's whimsical paintings and colorful wall constructions speak about our daily rituals as they relate to the state of constant change in which we live. In each painting and wall sculpture, abstract shapes invite a playful and thoughtful exchange by engaging the viewer through the freewheeling activity of our unconscious imagination.

Her work is collected both here and abroad and has been seen in such galleries as Stella Polaris in Beverly Hills, Galerie Beau Lezard in Paris, France and Art Expo Los Angeles. Kahn was the solo exhibiting artist at the James A. Doolittle Theatre Gallery during Lily Tomlin's Los Angeles engagement of Tomlin's one-woman play *The Search for Signs of Intelligent Life in the Universe*

For information contact ART LIVE: (818) 789-6091.

Beckie Kravetz

Masks

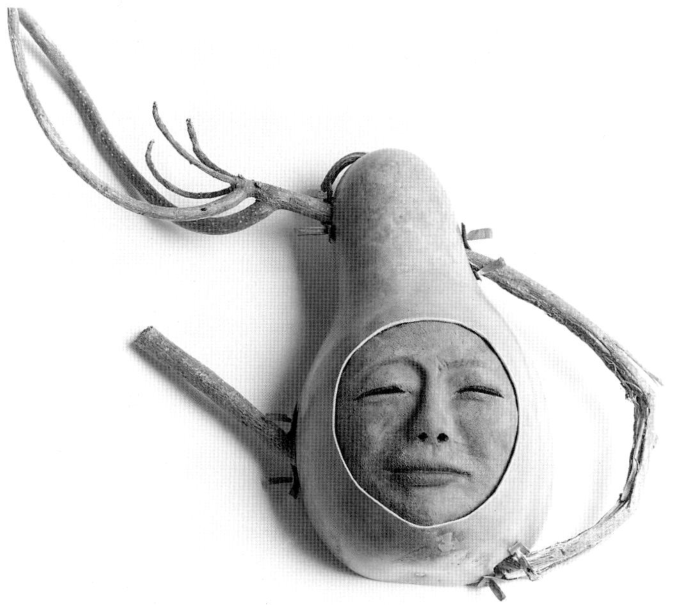

The Bering Strait to where . . ., (wall piece), leather face in gourd with wood, 18 x 15 x 85" (45" diagonal). Photo: Richard Trimarchi

Beckie Kravetz began creating masks for theater and continues her work as resident maskmaker for the Los Angeles Music Center Opera. Many of her works have a sense of playfulness and theatricality, the bright colors and exaggerated expressions of imaginary stage characters. Kravetz also creates masks using found organic materials. These faces exude a sense of calm and connection with the earth. Some of her work expands into full-scale sculpture, incorporating wood, leather, fabric and metal. These form box environments, figures or fountains that contain and contextualize the faces.

Kravetz's work has been seen at the Jewish Contemporary Museum in San Francisco and the Lincoln Center Performing Arts Library in New York City. She recently received a California Arts Council grant for artists working in special communities.

Commissions accepted.

Kravetz's work can be seen at Gallery 10, Scottsdale, AZ (602) 994-0405.

Studio visits by appointment. Call for address and directions: (310) 301-9189.

Linda Jacobson

Painting

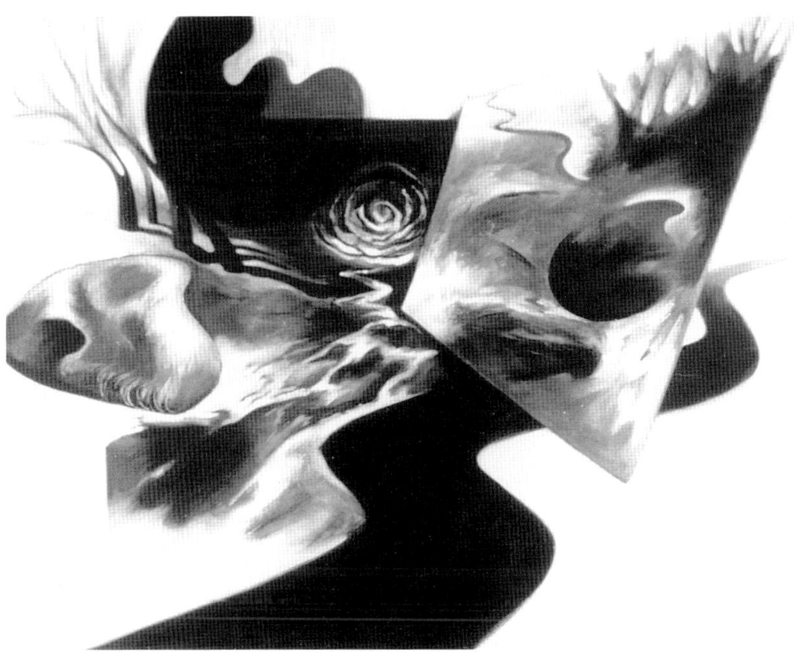

Black Pathway with Mirror, oil on canvas, 36 x 48"

Linda Jacobson's paintings explore emotional, psychological and spiritual dimensions of self as symbolized by landscape. They use nature as metaphor for psychic and spiritual states of consciousness. Her longterm involvement with mysticism, dream work, meditation and ritual, as well as her international teaching and travels are the source of her visionary images.

Widely exhibited, Jacobson's work is included in numerous public and private collections. During her Artist-in-Residence Fellowship at Dorland Mountain Arts Colony, she created paintings fusing landscape, depth psychology and mysticism. which were the genesis for her popular UCLA Extension courses: *Art as Transformation, Visionary Drawing*, and *Art & Spirit*. For these she was chosen Instructor of the Year.

Born in Los Angeles, Jacobson graduated *summa cum laude* from Art Center College of Design .

Commissions accepted.

Studio visits by appointment: (310) 822-6330.

Douglas Meyer

Painting

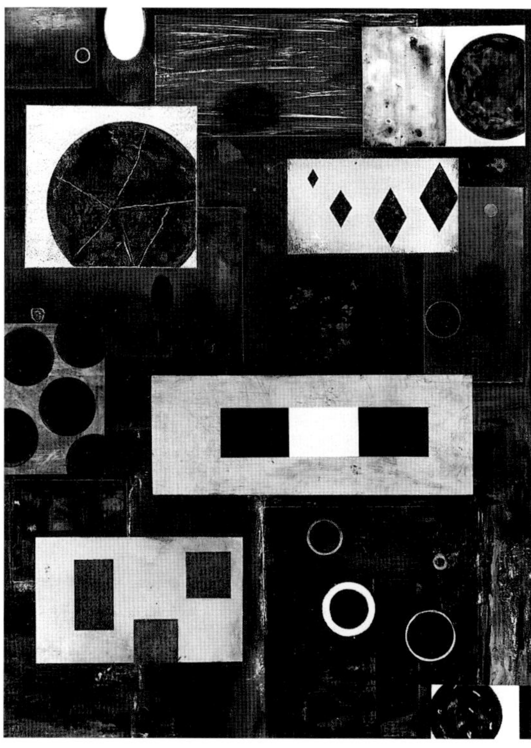

Emergence and Darkness, acrylic on canvas, 16 x 12"

Creating structure on the edge of chaos is a theme that weaves through the paintings, prints, and watercolors of Douglas Meyer. His artwork resonates with self-similar geometric orderings held together in fields of organic color. The rich and varied surfaces he creates have a physical presence that is powerfully seductive.

Douglas Meyer's work has been exhibited locally and nationally in galleries and museums. He is included in many private collections. His public/corporate collections include the U.S. State Department, Eli Broad/Sun America, First Los Angeles Bank, Nestle Inc. and Bank of America.

Commissions accepted.

Meyer's work can be seen at William Turner Gallery, Venice, (310) 392-8399.

Studio visits by appointment: (310) 822-4038. His studio is located at 2922 Beach Avenue, Venice, CA 90291.

Curtis Ripley

Painting

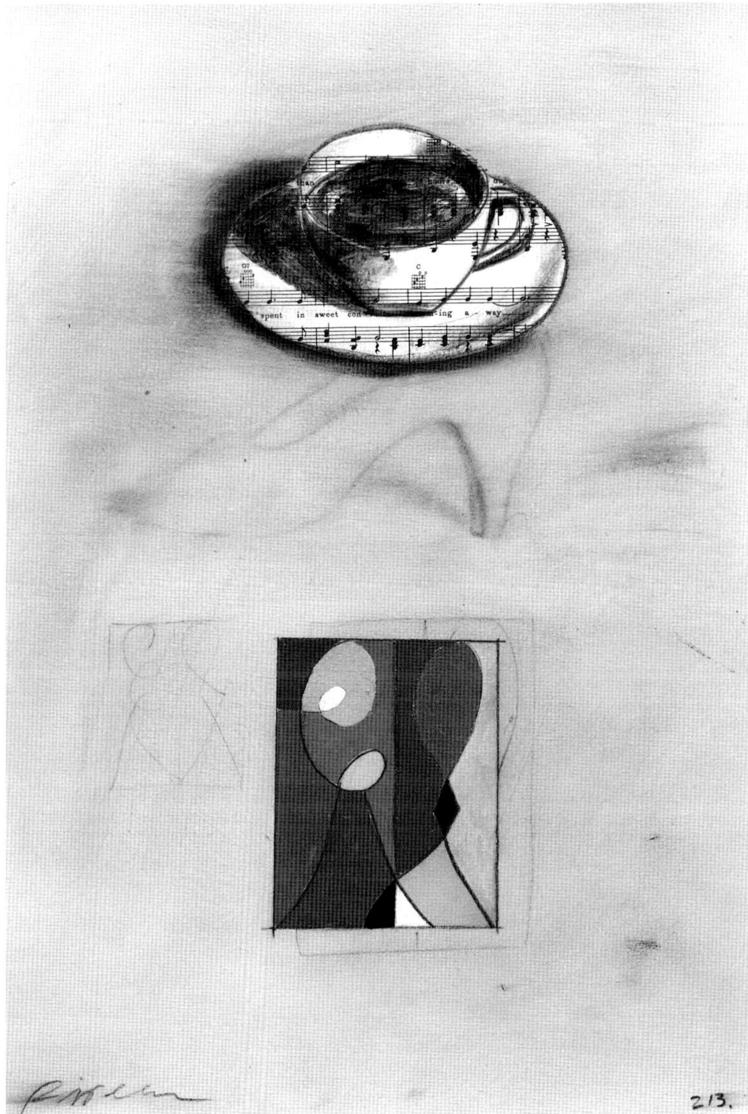

Page 213, pencil, collage and oil on paper, 21 x 15". Photo: Susan Einstein

Commissions accepted.

Studio visits by appointment: (310) 396-8026. Ripley's studio is located at 201 San Juan Avenue, Venice, CA 90291.

Pamela Leeds

Photography / Sculpture

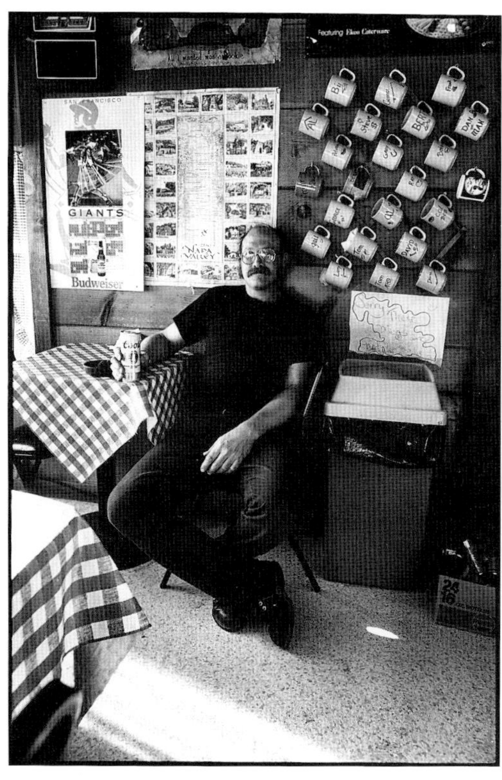

Soda Canyon Regular
black and white
silver gelatin print
8 x 12" image, 11 x 14" paper

Via photography and sculptural works, Pamela Leeds explores the impact and significance of human associations, environments and objects that indelibly effect our basic need for acknowledgment of personal growth and existence. Themes of *choice* and *change* underlie much of the work.

Leeds' work includes black and white, color and hand-colored photography, three-dimensional photoworks, intimate sculptural objects, artist's *books*, and large-scale photo/object/text installations. Since receiving her M.F.A. from Claremont Graduate School in 1990, her work has been seen in numerous exhibitions and is in private collections across the U.S. Call for current exhibition venues and dates.

Visits to Pamela Leeds' studio may be arranged by appointment. Call for address and directions: (310) 822-2317. Mail may be sent to: Pamela Leeds Fine Art, 2554 Lincoln Boulevard, Suite 770, Venice, CA 90291.

Betty Gold

Sculpture

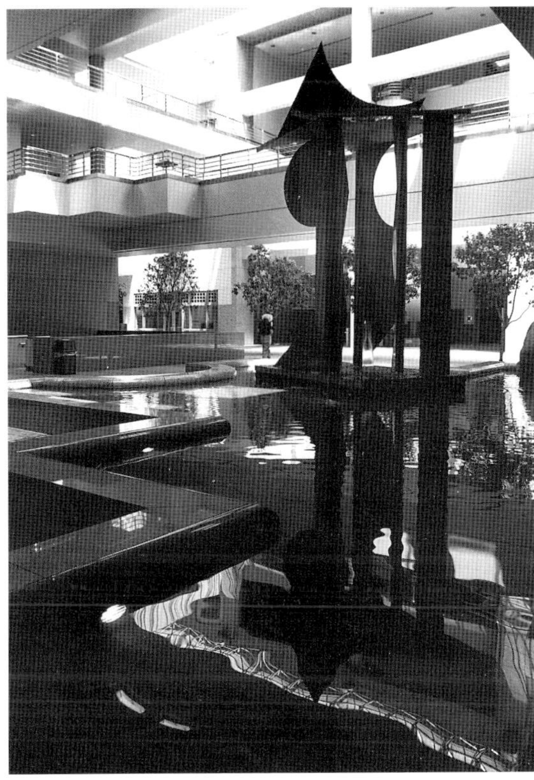

Redwood Moonrise, Fountain #1
stainless steel and water
23 x 14 x 8'
Photo: Betty Gold

I have been a professional sculptor for more than 25 years. I work in diverse media to create pieces that reflect my artistic focus on intensifying opposites, such as the contrast of my rugged, oversized sandblasted, outdoor steel sculpture with my indoor, delicate, gold-leaf icon visuals.
— Betty Gold

Gold's work appears in permanent installations and private collections throughout the world -- Seoul, Korea; Sayo, Japan; Mexico City, Mexico -- and is installed at major museums, universities and public buildings throughout the country.
Commissions accepted.

Gold's work can be seen at Nemiroff Deutsch Fine Art, Santa Monica, (310) 315-5400; La Quinta Sculpture Park, La Quinta (619) 564-6464; and ARTyard, Denver, CO, (303) 777-3219.

Studio visits by appointment: (310) 399-5205. Her studio is located at 1324 Pacific Avenue, Venice CA 90291.

Judy Stabile

Sculpture

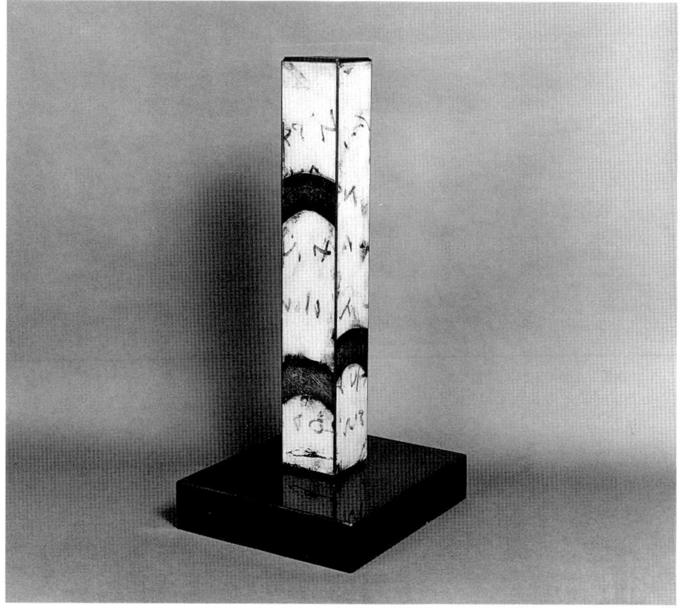

Wish List, gold leaf with glass and enamel 24 x 3 3/4" square, 15 x 13" granite base. Photo: Tom Randolph

Judy Stabile is best known for her unconventional use of materials in her approach to painting. Using multiple layers of gold, silver, copper leaf and coated paint on the back of glass, she integrates a geometric dialogue with a human, emotional side. Her well versed cone and cylinder series now gives rise to a more vulnerable imagery and the written word.

Educated at Chouinard Art Institute in Los Angeles, Stabile lives and works in her studio in Venice. Her work has been shown at the Long Beach Museum of Art and Laguna Art Museum, and is represented in many corporate and private collections in the U.S. and abroad including Atlantic Richfield, NY; Cedars- Sinai, Los Angeles; and Daniel Melnick, Los Angeles. Her commissions include Hewlett Packard, London, and Hyatt Regency, Paris.

Stabile's work can be seen at Nemiroff Deutsch Fine Art, Los Angeles, (310) 315-5400; Valerie Miller Fine Art, Palm Desert, (619) 773-4483; Judy Kay and Associates, San Francisco, (415) 421-3933; and Elizabeth Michaels, Falls Church, VA, (703) 256-6395.

Studio visits by appointment: (310) 399-0183.

Nana K. Varnedoe

Sculpture

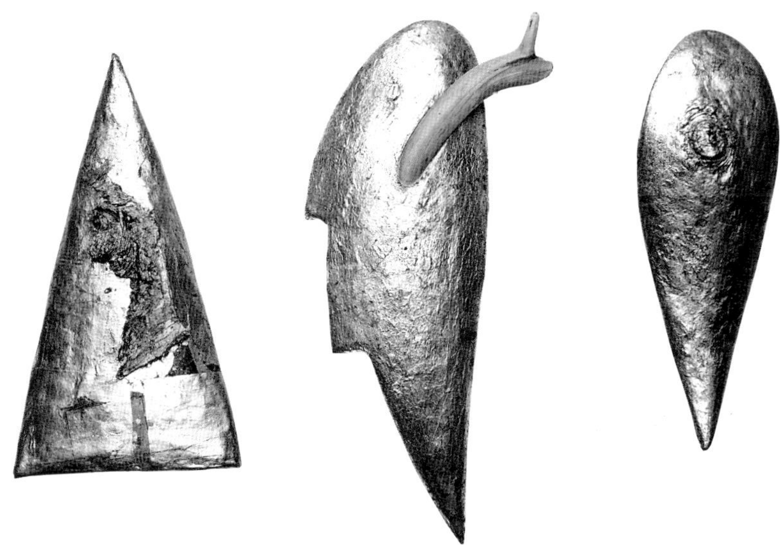

Keltoid, paper maché, wood, gold leaf, bark, 20 x 28 x 3". Photo: Georgia Hodges

Nana Varnedoe has long been interested in ancient cultures and the mysteries and spirituality which speak to all ages, bridging past and present. As human beings have searched for a means of describing the intangible, these mysteries found their way into artistic expression in ancient times much as they do in today's intensely modern world.

Materials are chosen for their richness and texture. Some are suggestive of centuries of decaying gold and linen wrappings, of patinaed metals and crumbling stone, contrasting with modern urban materials such as lead, steel and rubber. Works vary in size and include both wall-hung and free-standing pieces.

Varnedoe has exhibited and lectured internationally and is spending part of 1994 as Artist-in-Residence in Pont-Aven, Brittany, France.

Media: Stone, metal wood, paper maché.

Studio visits by appointment: (310) 392-6573. Her studio is located at 320A Sunset Avenue, Venice, CA 90291.

Oscar J. Martinez

Mixed Media

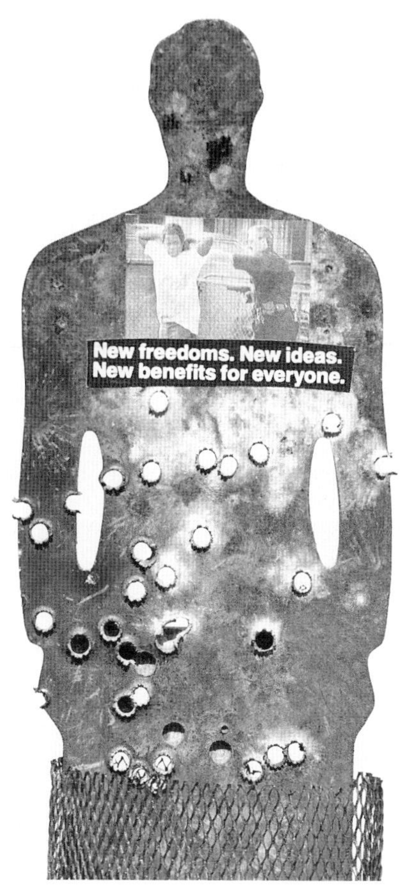

New Freedoms (detail)
steel, collage, text, lifesize
Photo: Oscar J. Martinez

My art is not born easily. It is as much about the process of creation as it is about any subject matter. Its creation is an emotional, philosophical and physical struggle; and the work often reveals this in its surfaces. My subject matter is generally a reaction to the external forces in my life. Religion and politics, taboo subjects in conversation with a stranger, are subjects I often take up with the viewer.

As an artist, my eyes have only begun to open. The work I present is what I see when I close them back up. — Oscar J. Martinez

Martinez's work can be seen at LA Artcore, Los Angeles, (213) 617-3274.

Studio visits by appointment: (909) 598-8832.

Peter Mark Richman

Painting

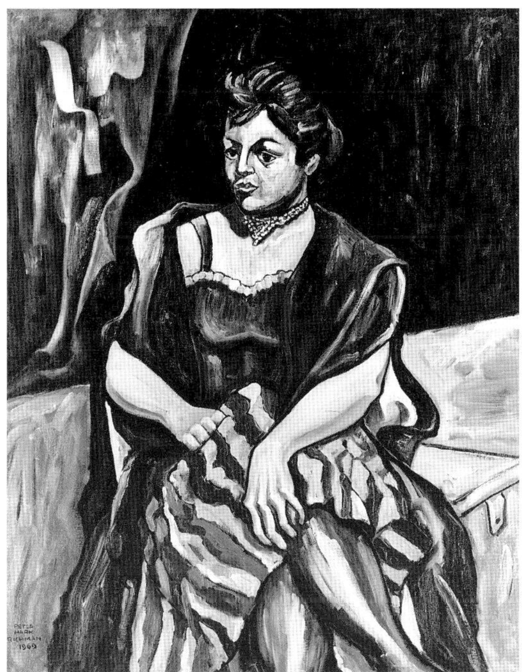

Indian Stunt Girl, oil on canvas, 37 x 26"

An artist has something in him that has to be expressed. The way he expresses himself on canvas or paper is relative to his inner life. I believe in a spiritual sense. The artist has very little choice in the matter. No matter what he does, what comes out is really him in certain periods of his life. It is constantly changing. — Peter Mark Richman

Richman has had a dual career as a painter and actor all of his adult life. He came to Hollywood from Broadway to do his first film, the memorable *Friendly Persuasion*, with Gary Cooper. He went on to appear in innumerable stage, film and television roles including his own TV series, *Cain's Hundred*, and subsequent series, *Dynasty*, *Three's Company* and *Santa Barbara*.

He has exhibited widely and is represented in hundreds of collections, including the permanent collection of the Crocker Museum in Sacramento, and the University of the State of New York at Albany. Commissions accepted.

Studio visits by appointment. Call for address and directions: (213) 964-1871.

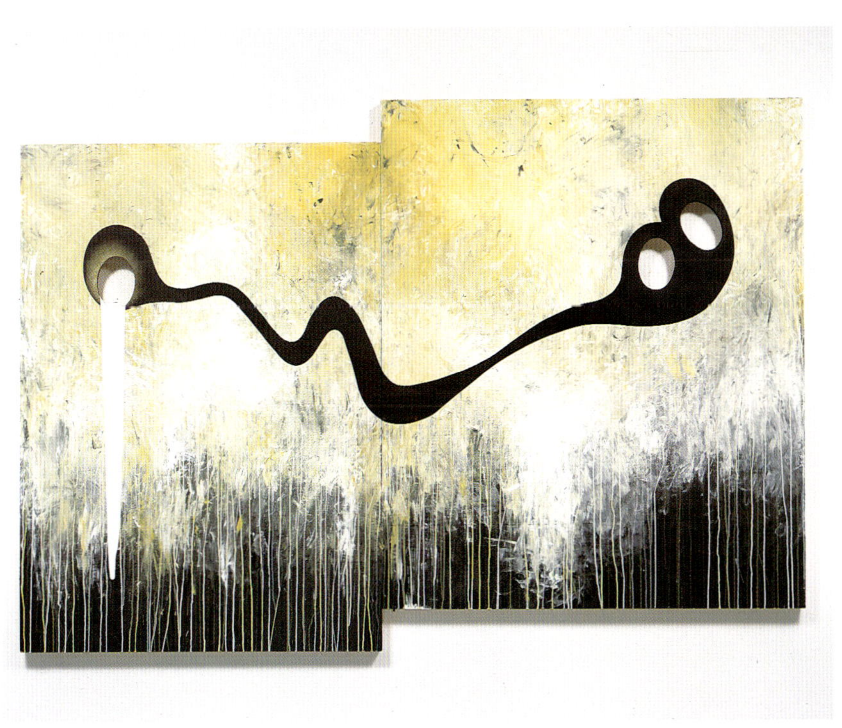

Lisa Adams

Drain, acrylic on wood, 65 x 96". Photo: Gene Ogami

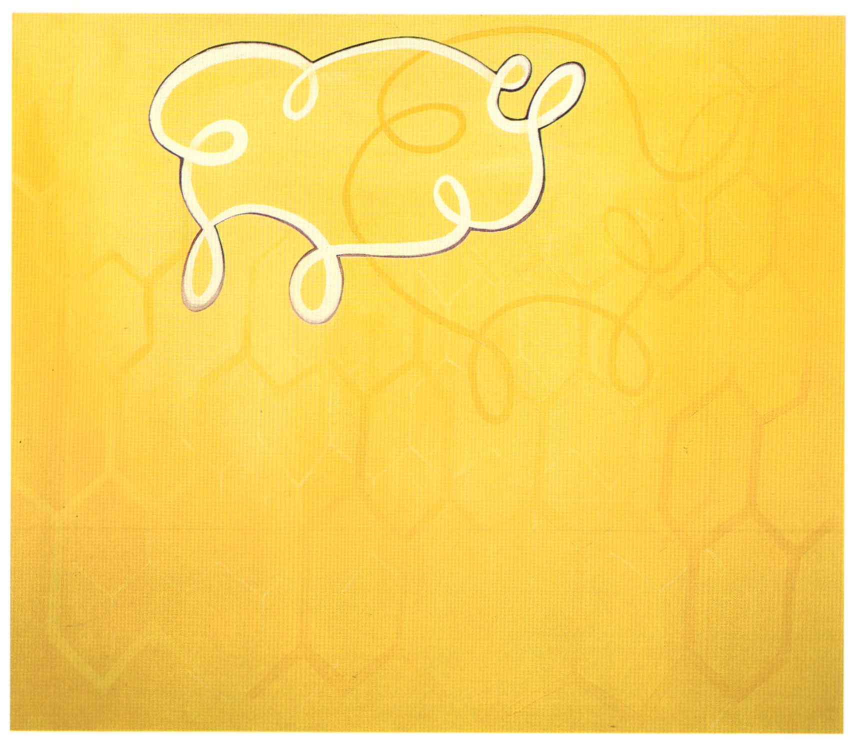

Dawn Arrowsmith

Closer to the Sun oil on wood panel, 60 x 72". Photo: Gene Ogami

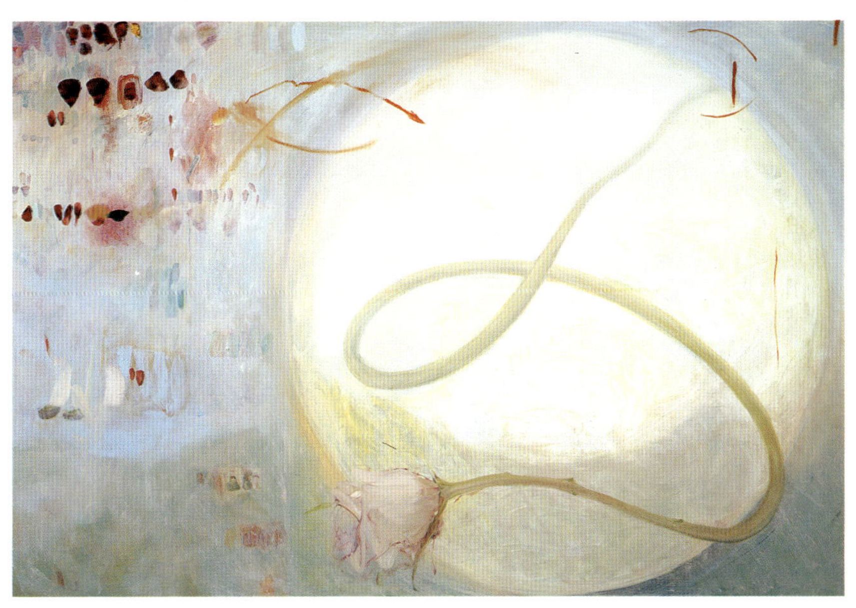

Ciel Bergman aka Cheryl Bowers

Moon I (Rose-Headed Snake), oil, wax and alkyd, 49 x 60". Photo: William Dewey

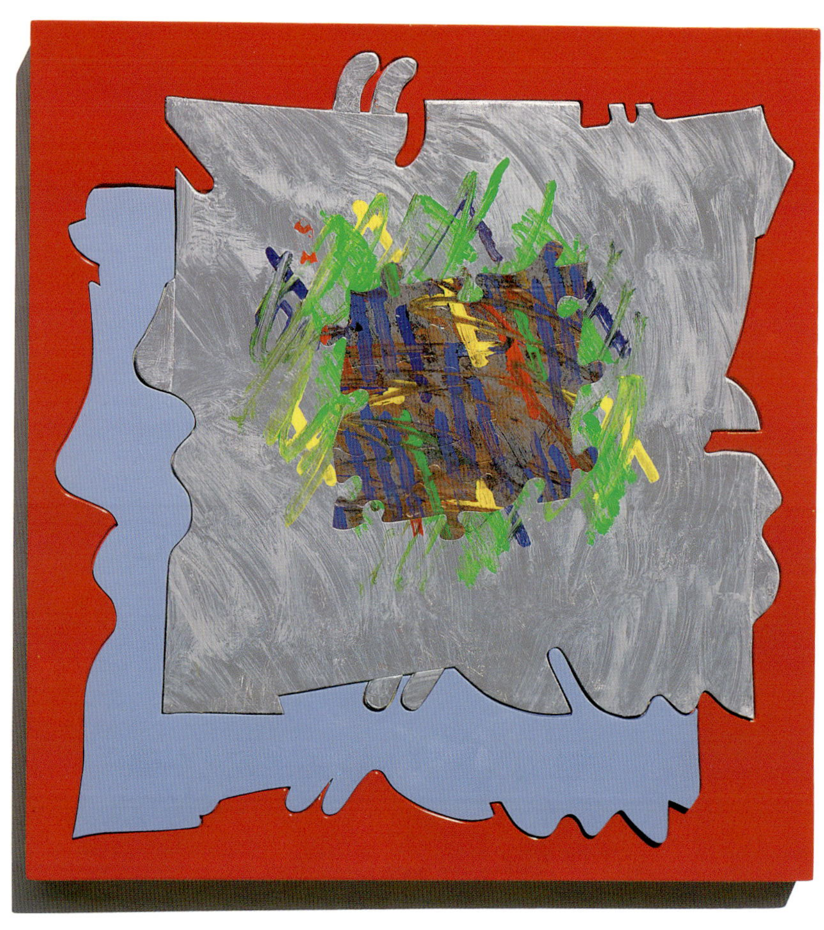

Alan Blizzárd

Broken Arrow #29, Shadow Box #2, rhoplex and oil on canvas and wood, 33 x 32"

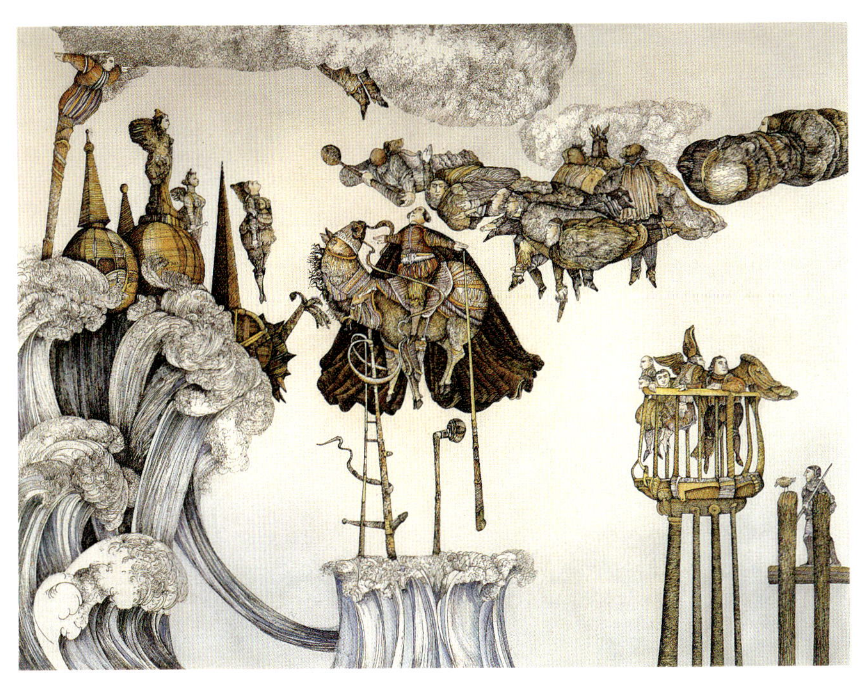

Zevi Blum

Protocols and Easements, etching and watercolor, 18 x 24″

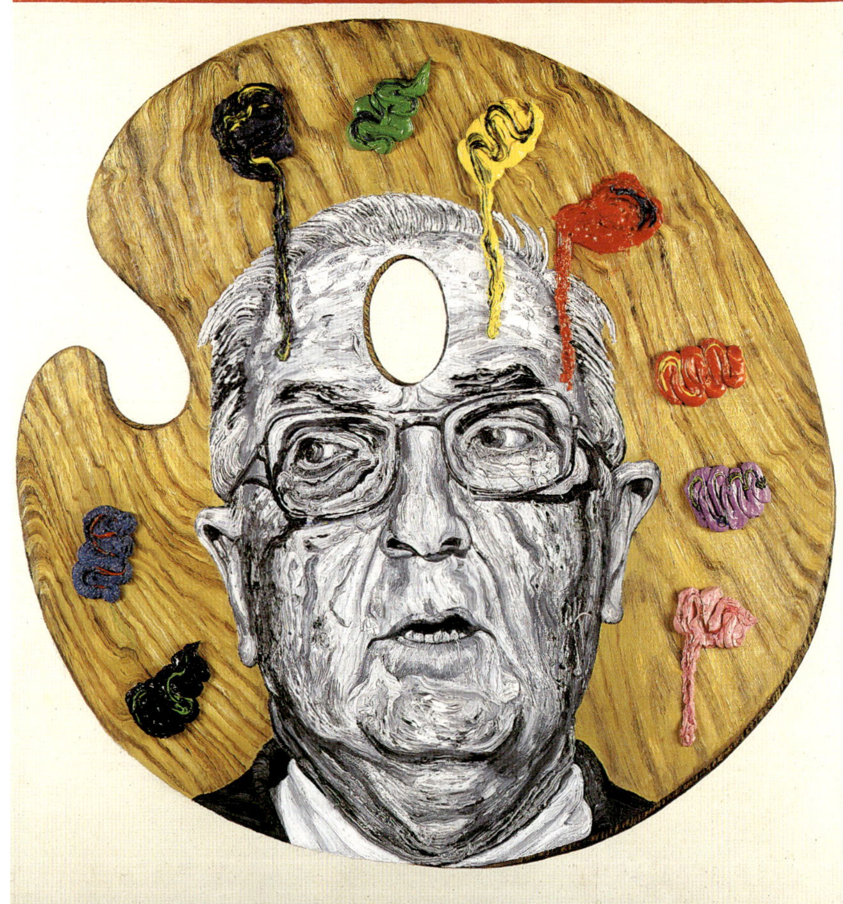

Robbie Conal

Artificial Art Official (Jesse Helms), oil on canvas, 53 x 42". Photo: Alan Shaffer

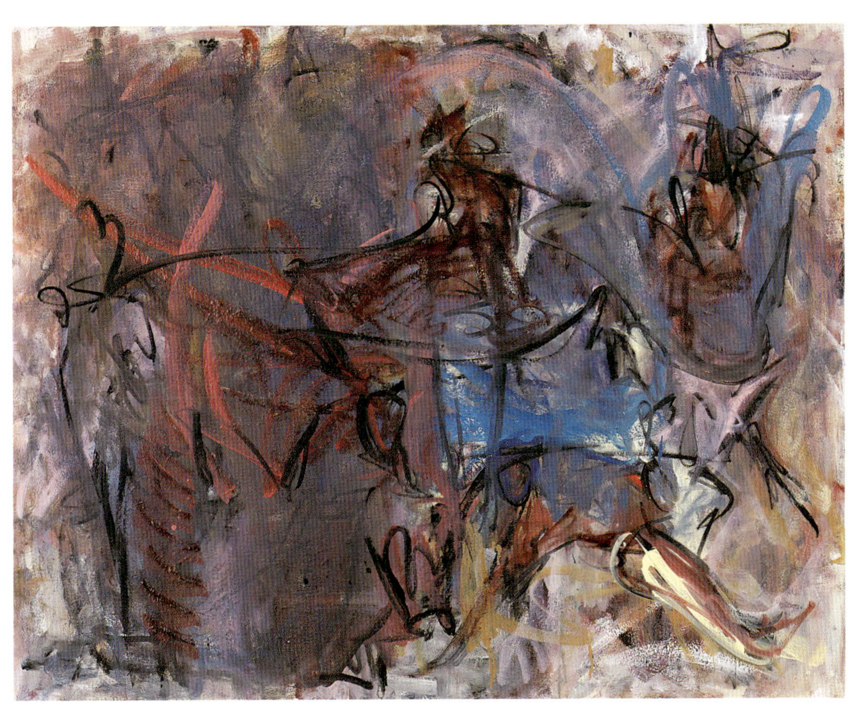

Katherine Coons

Red Passion II, enamel on canvas, 36 x 46". Photo: Scott Hensel

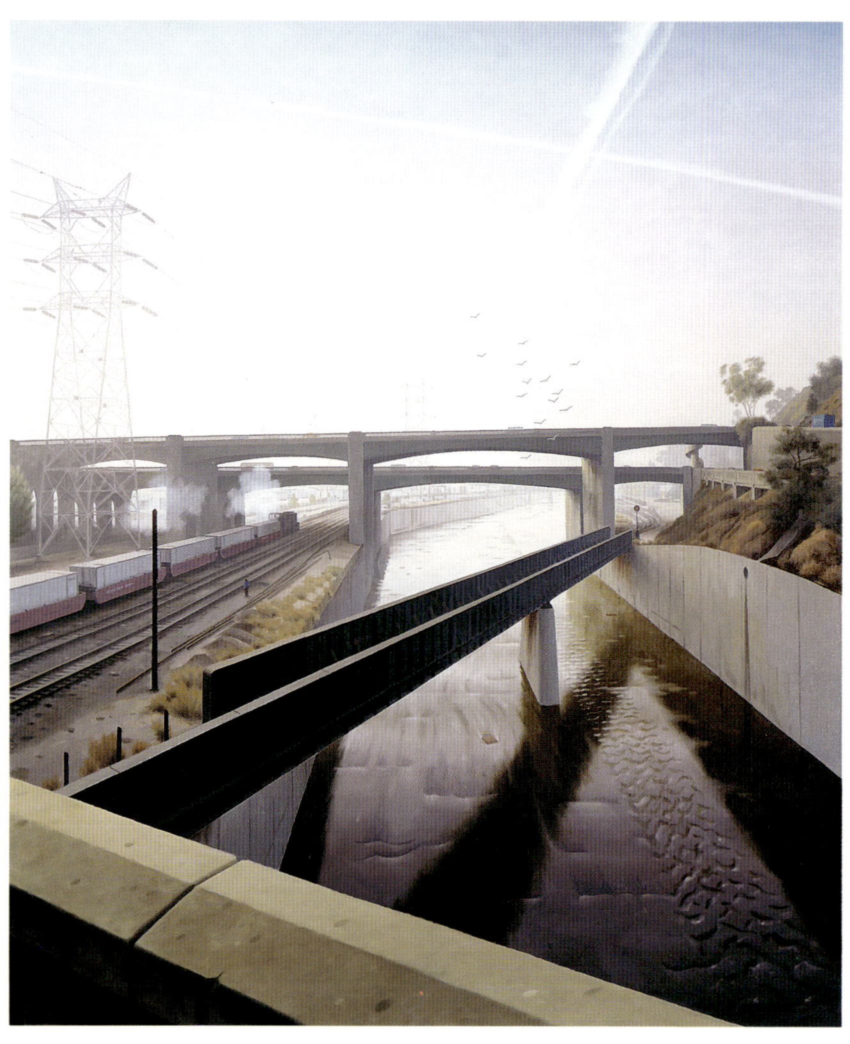

James Doolin

Connections, oil on canvas, 84 x 72". Photo: Brewer Photography

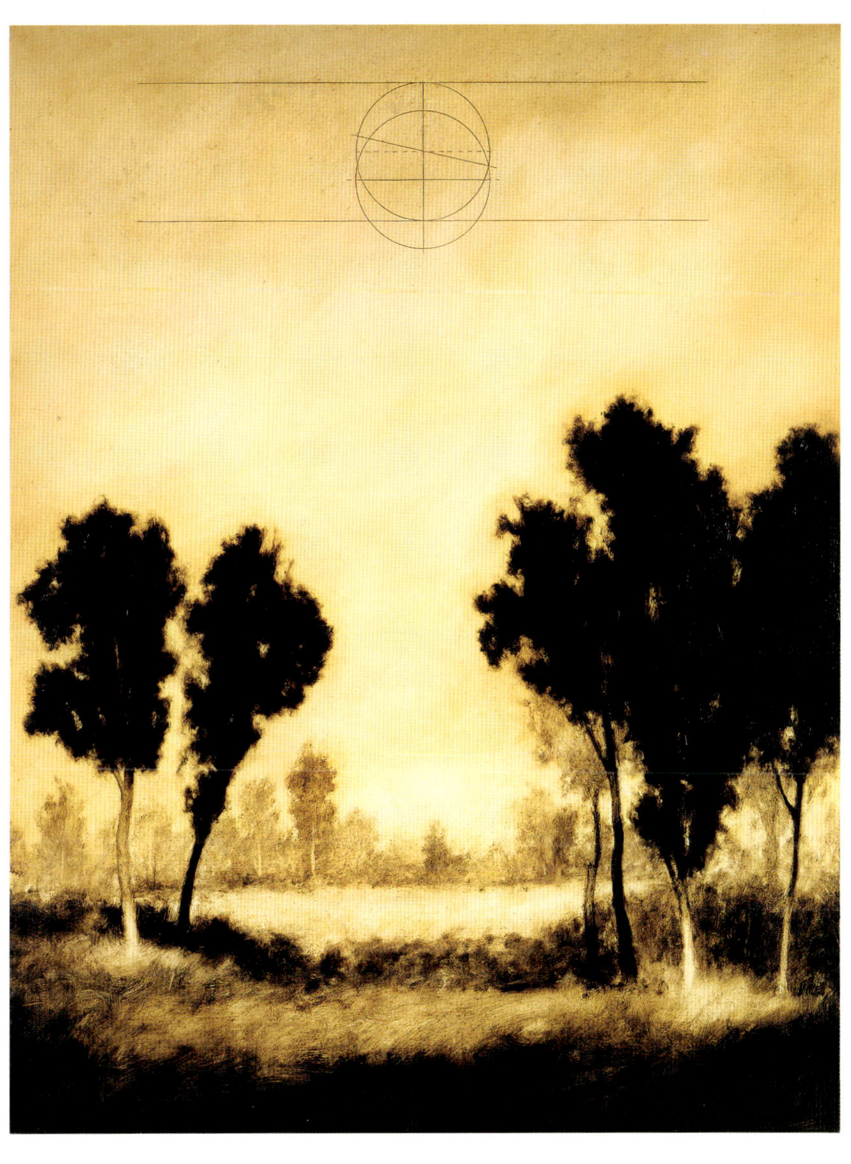

Brad Durham

Journey of Solitude, oil on canvas. 60 x 47 x 2 3/4"

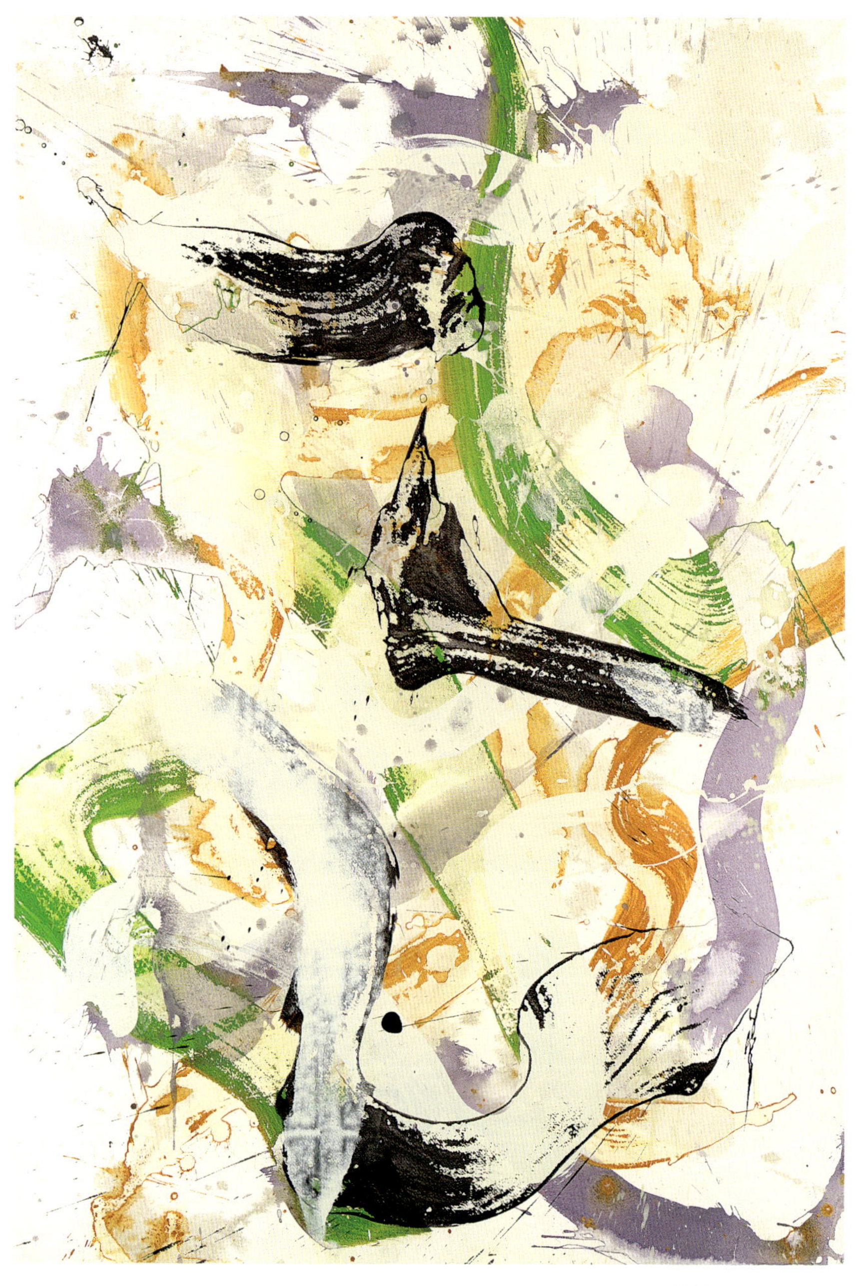

Gregory Wiley Edwards

The Profound Influence of a Fighter Group, Operations Man, acrylic on paper, 41 3/4 x 27 1/2"

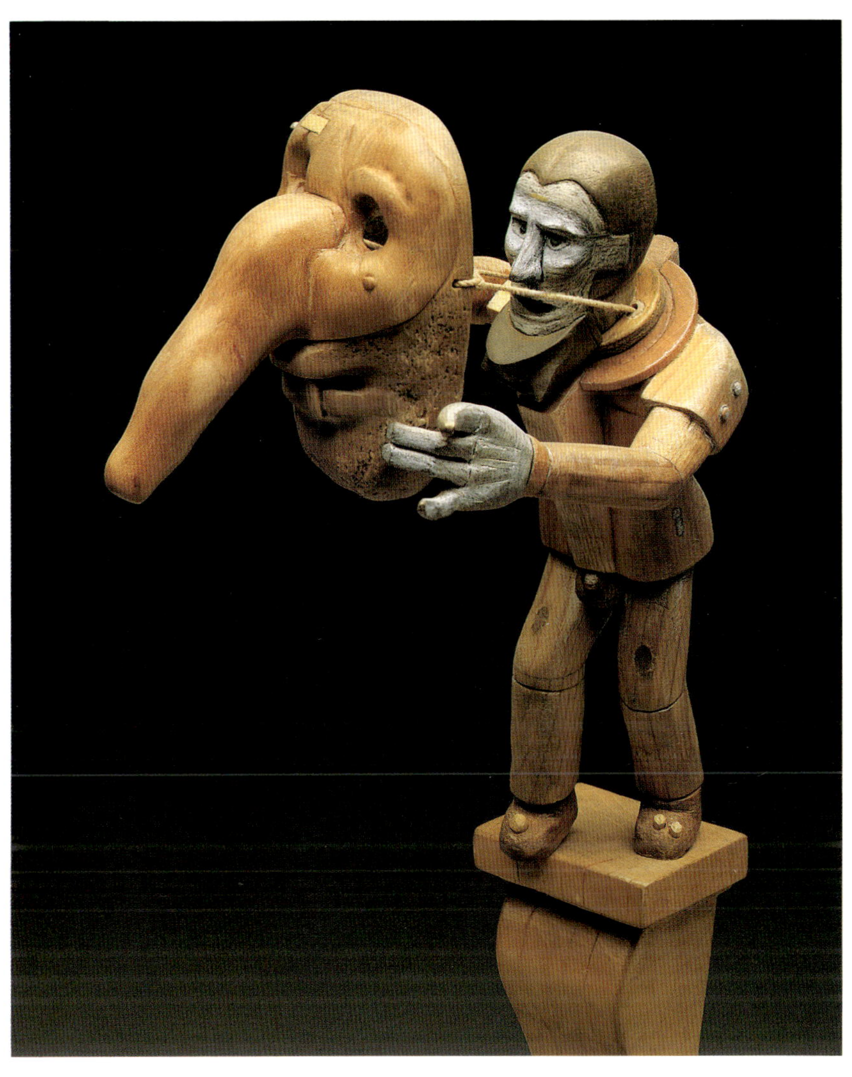

John F. Frame

Wormwood's View, (detail), wood, bronze pigment, 22 x 16 x 16". Photo: Douglas M. Parker

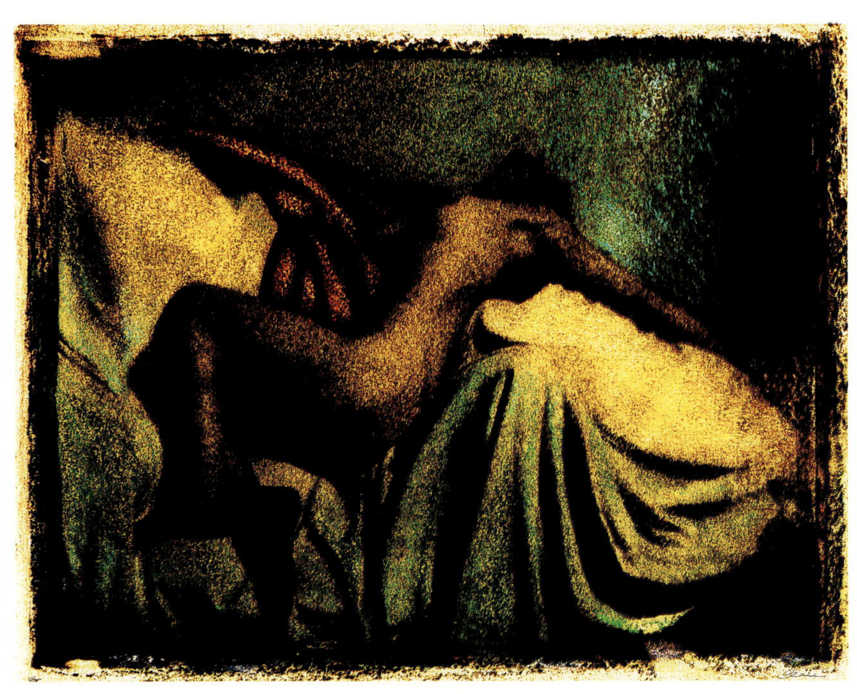

Ed Freeman

Untitled, chromogenic color print, 16 x 20"

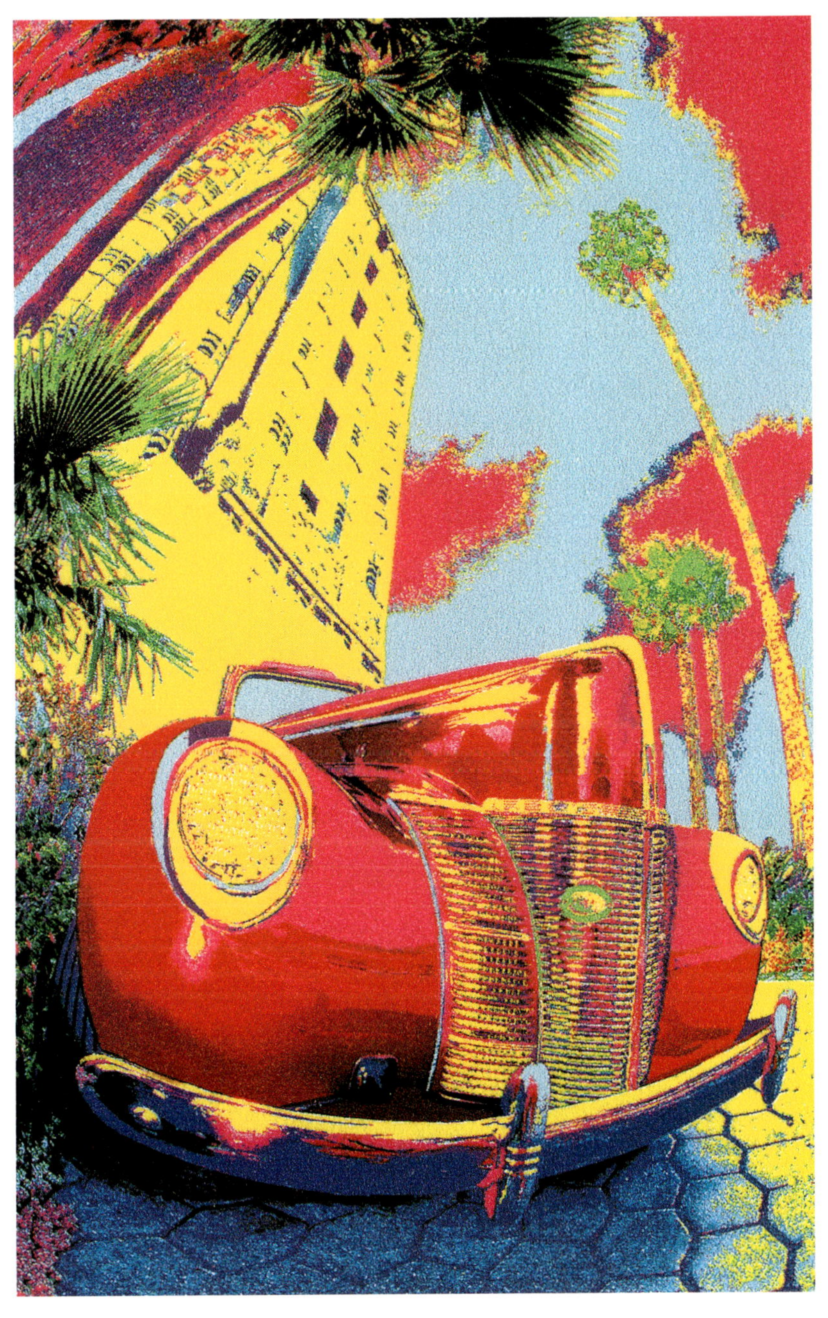

Jane Gottlieb

Friendly Ford, mixed media, 27 x 38"

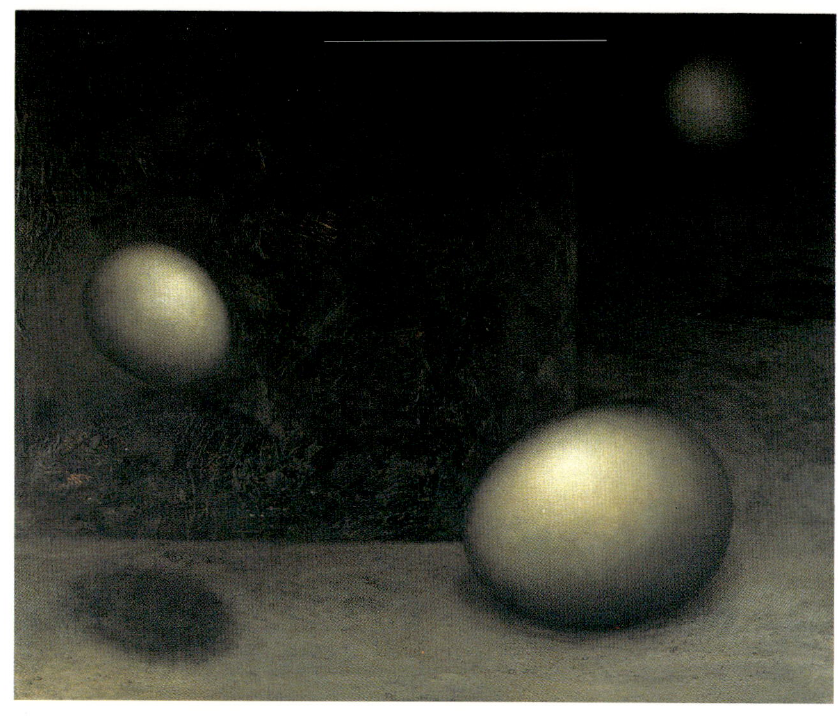

Janne M. Greibesland

Future Reminiscence, paper, sand, acrylic and oil on canvas, 5 1/2 x 6 1/2′

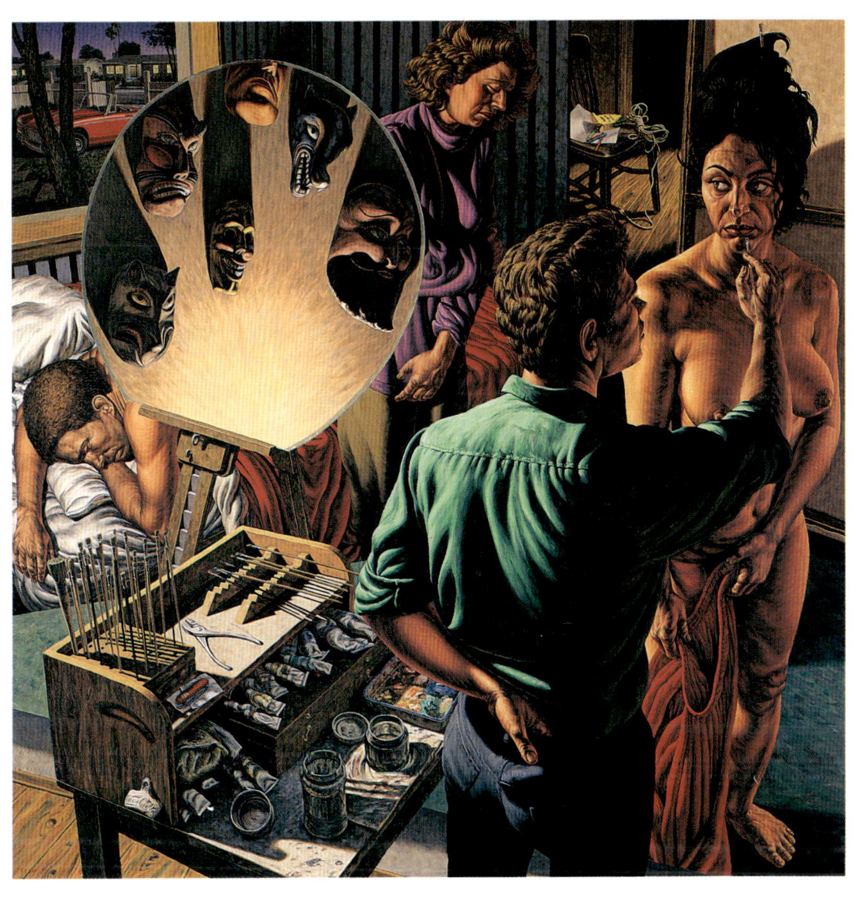

F. Scott Hess

At Arms Length, oil on canvas, 86 x 86". Courtesy Ovsey Gallery. Photo: Douglas M. Parker

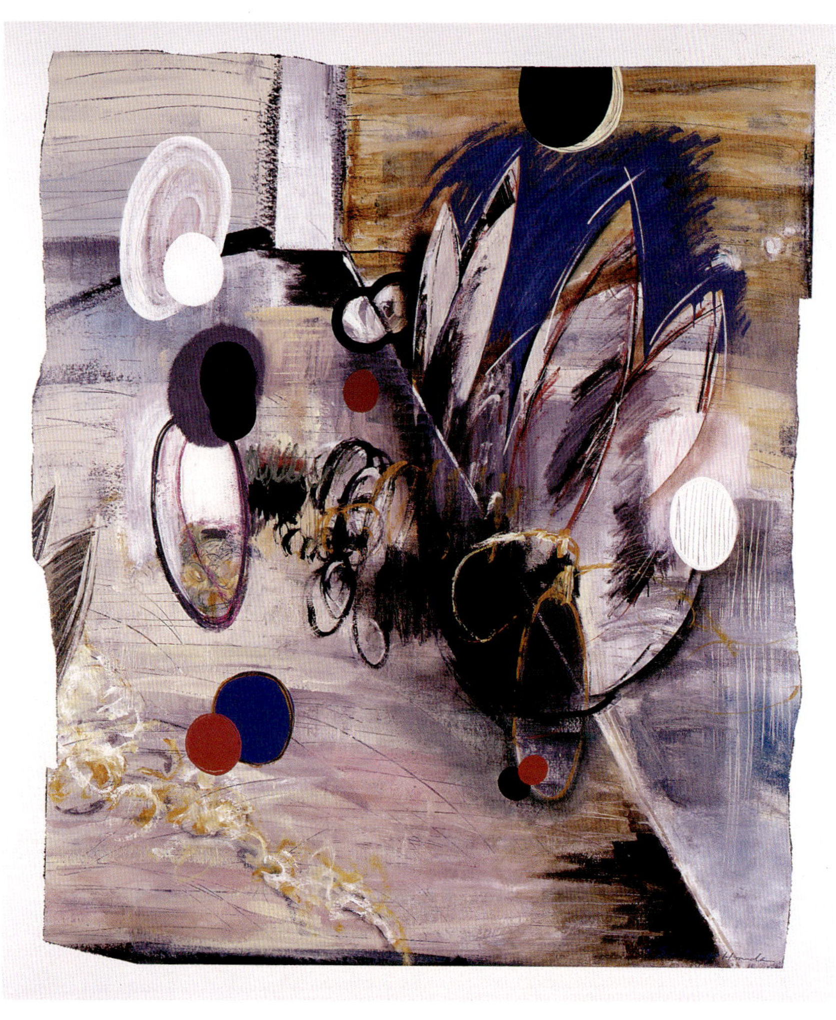

Shingo Honda

Case #44, acrylic on canvas, 71 x 63". Photo: Daniel Uppendahl

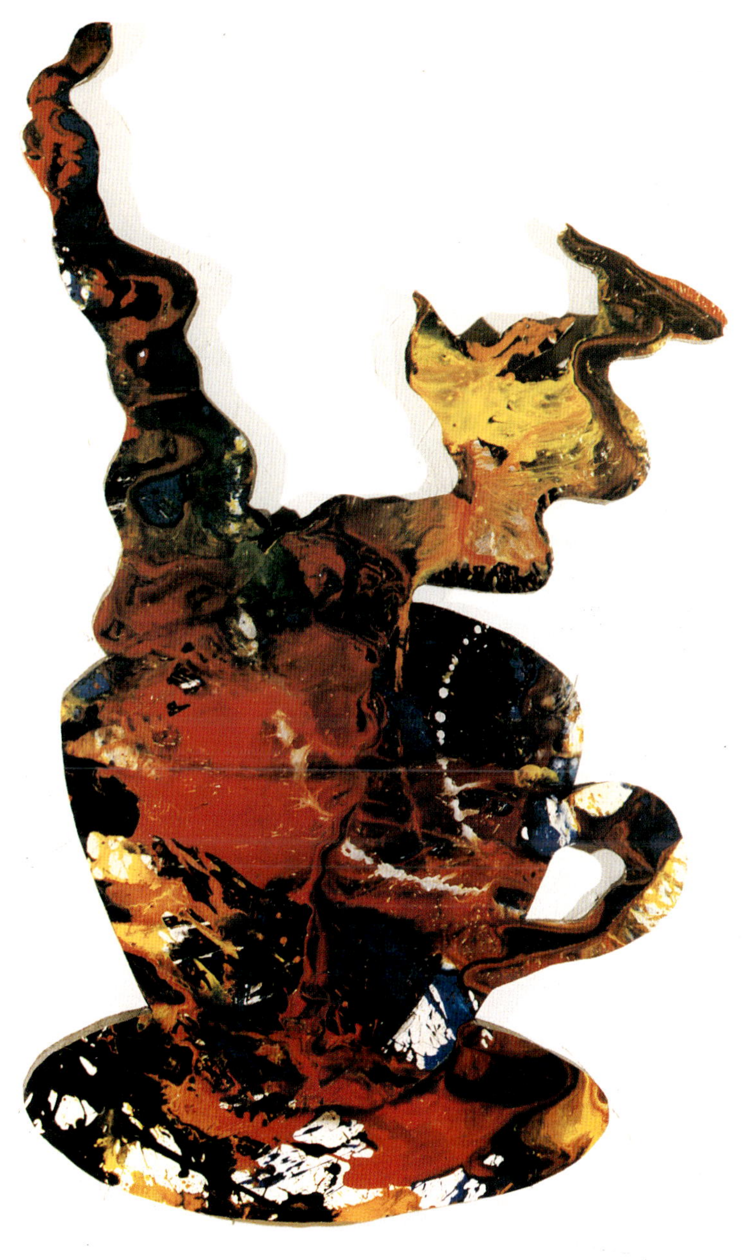

Jamy Kahn

High Spirits, series, acrylic and core board construction, 65 x 37 x 2"

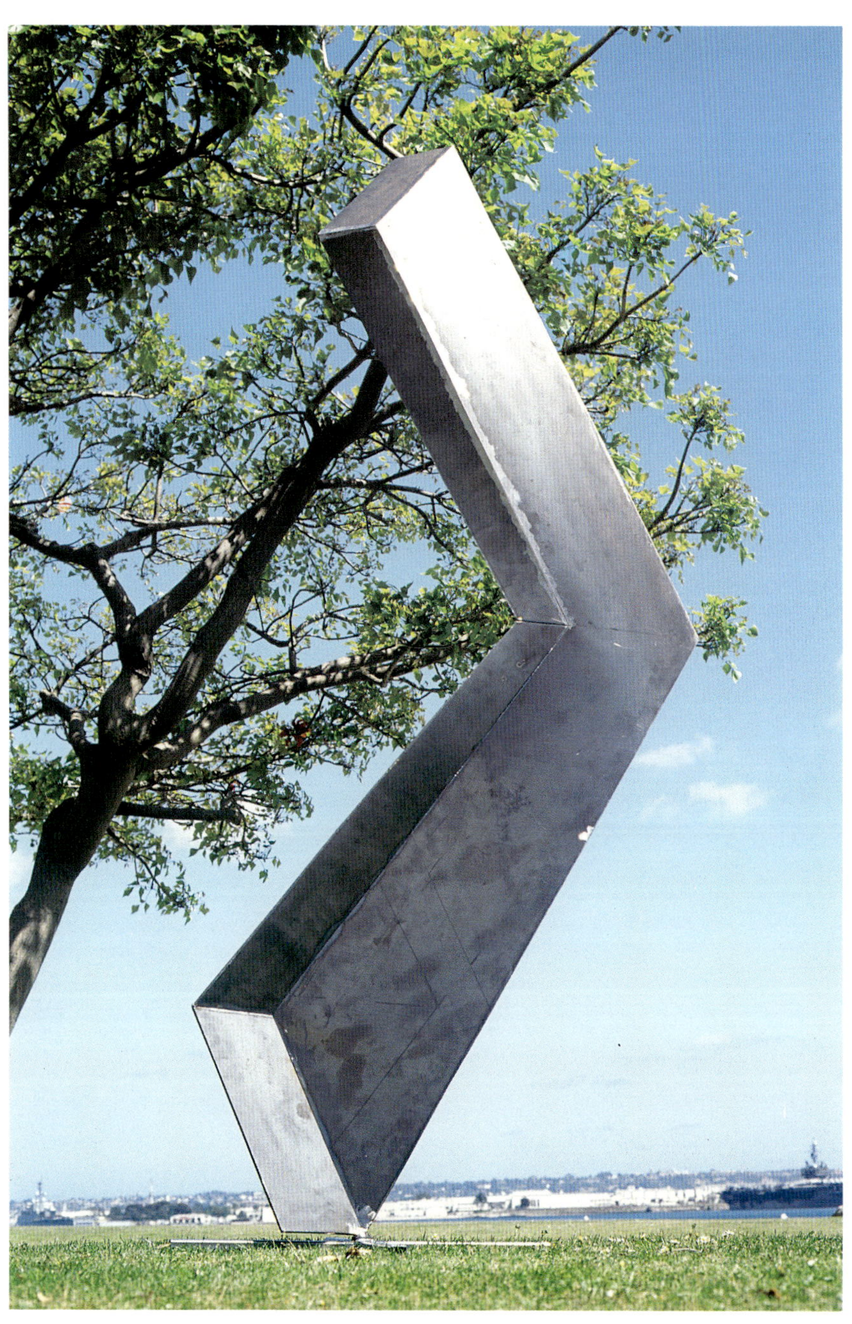

Jeffery Laudenslager

Huntress, steel, 7 x 3 x 1'

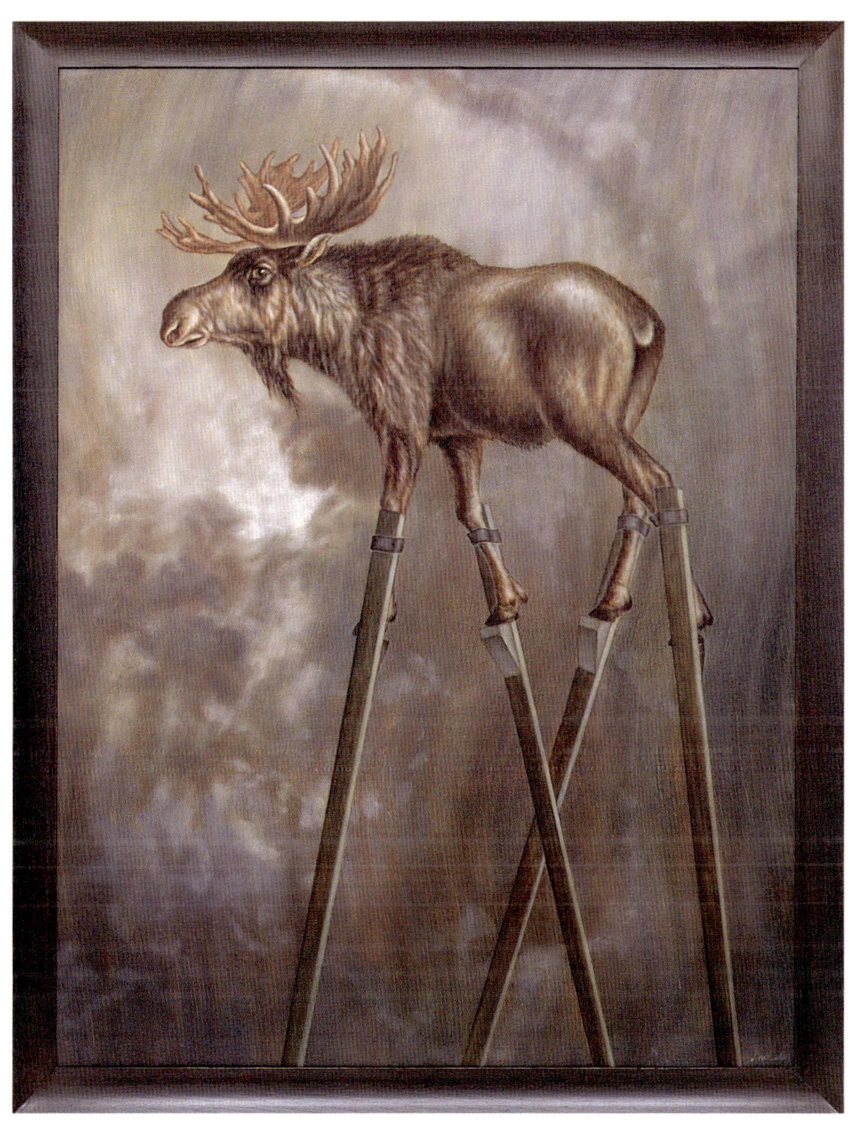

Randall Lavender

Moose on Stilts, oil on panel, 50 x 39". Photo: Susan Einstein

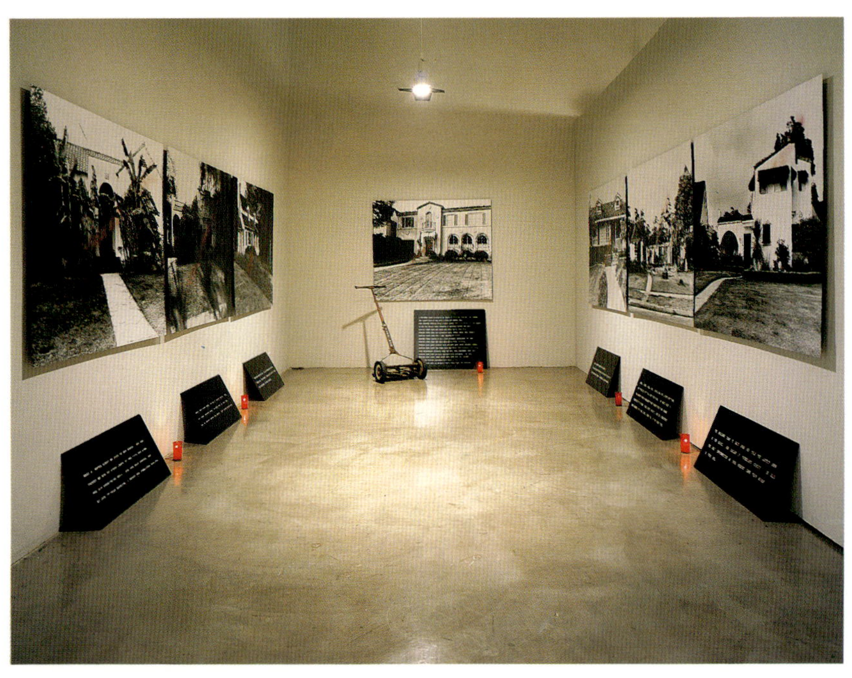

Pamela Leeds

Memory Block, photo installation, 11 x 16′, photographs (4 x 5′ each), text, objects

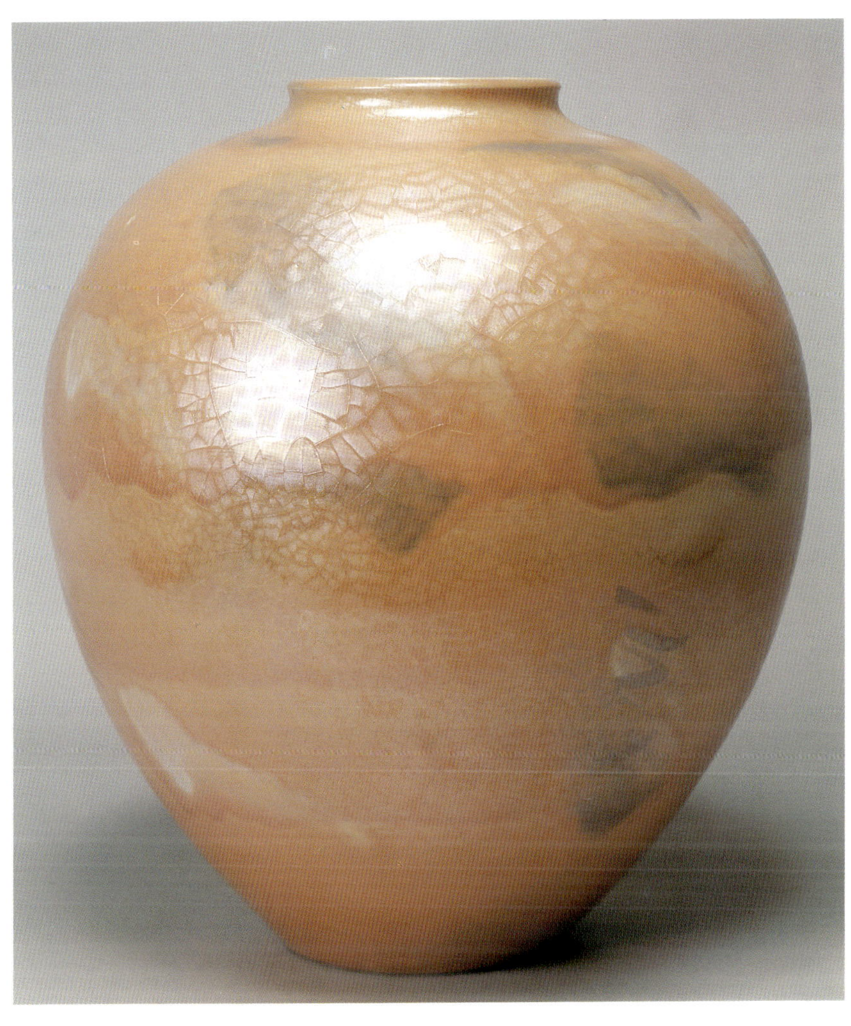

Gary McCloy

Round Jar / Coral & Smoke, wheel thrown, triple fired glaze, 22" diameter, 26" high
Photo: Gary McCloy

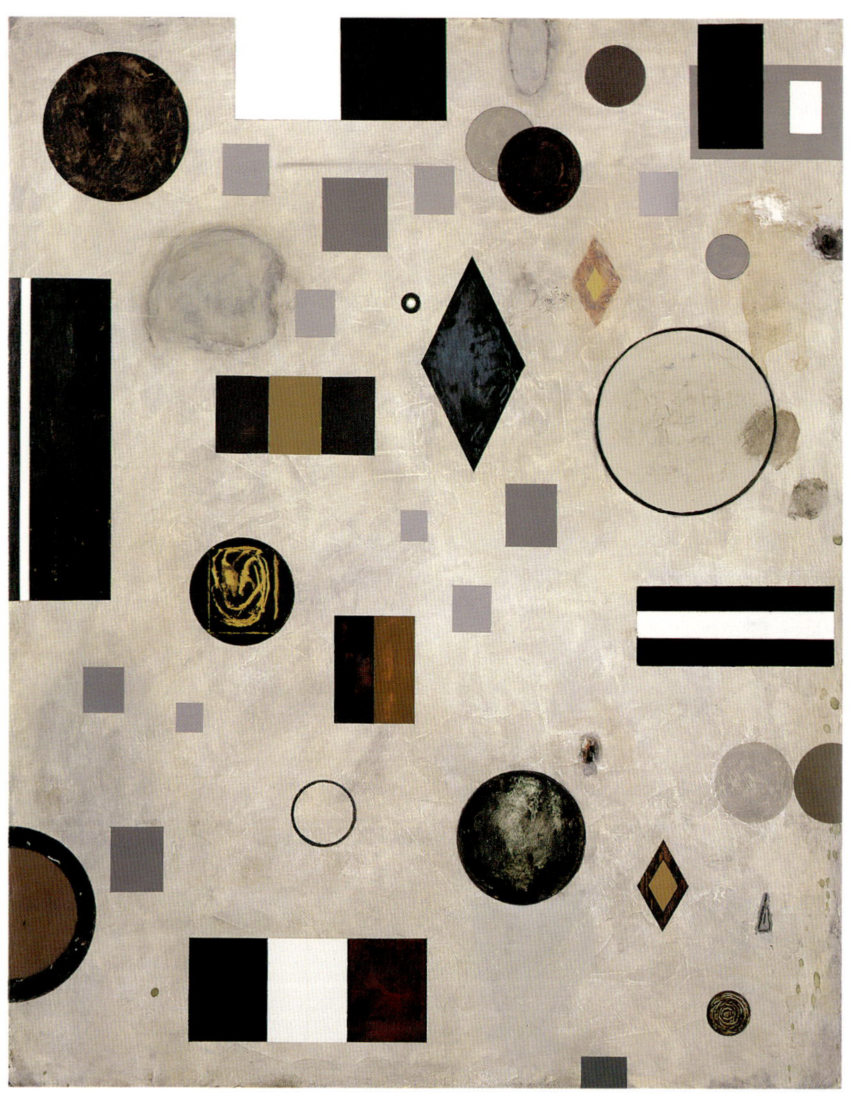

Douglas Meyer

Spanish Winter, acrylic on canvas, 20 x 16"

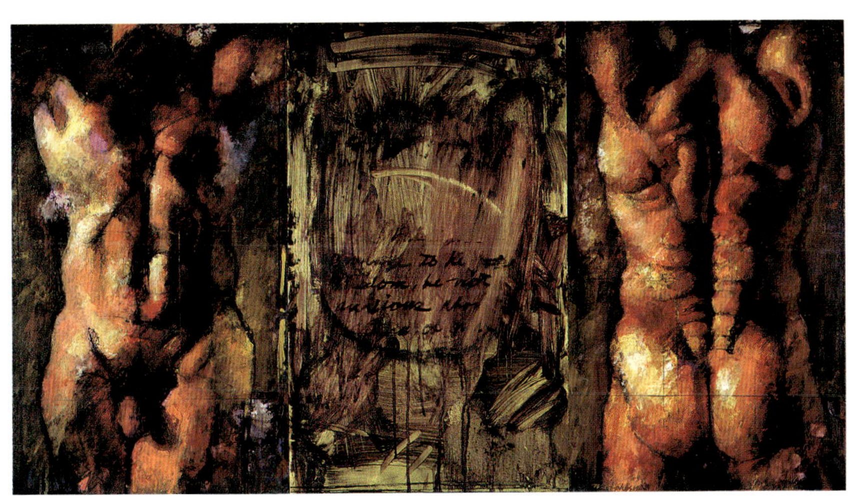

Jim Morphesis

Pericles Gate, oil, charcoal, and gold leaf on wood panel, 30 x 54". Photo: Kevin Noble

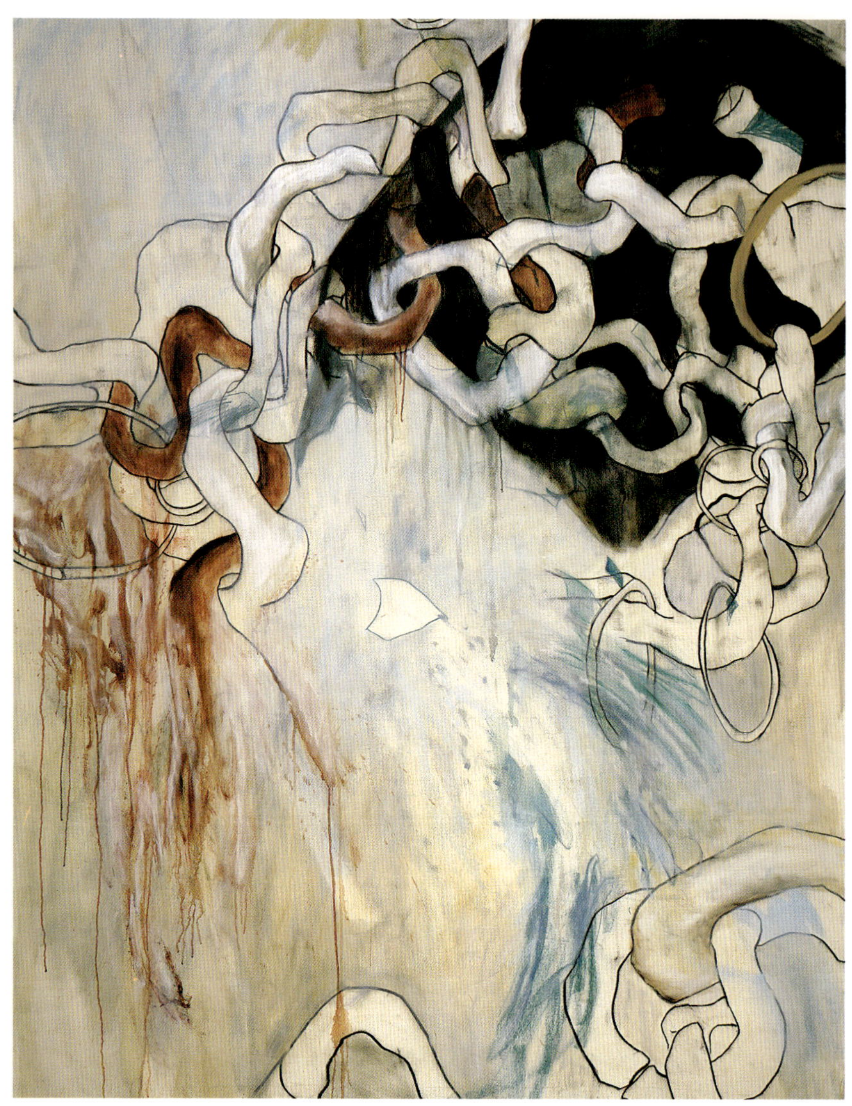

Laurel Paley

Links and Intervals: Bat Mitzvah, oil and drawing media on canvas, 84 x 67"
Photo: Robert Wedemeyer

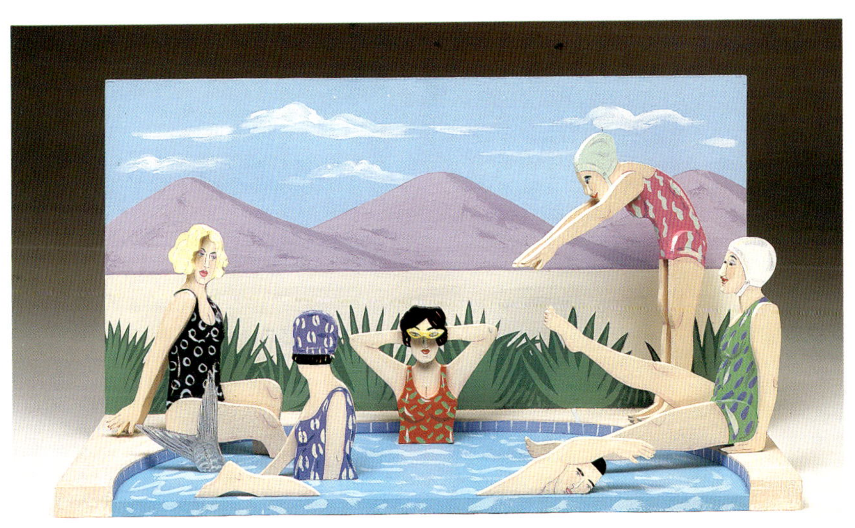

Laurie Pincus

Palm Springs Weekend, painted wood, 13 x 24 x 10". Photo: Douglas M. Parker

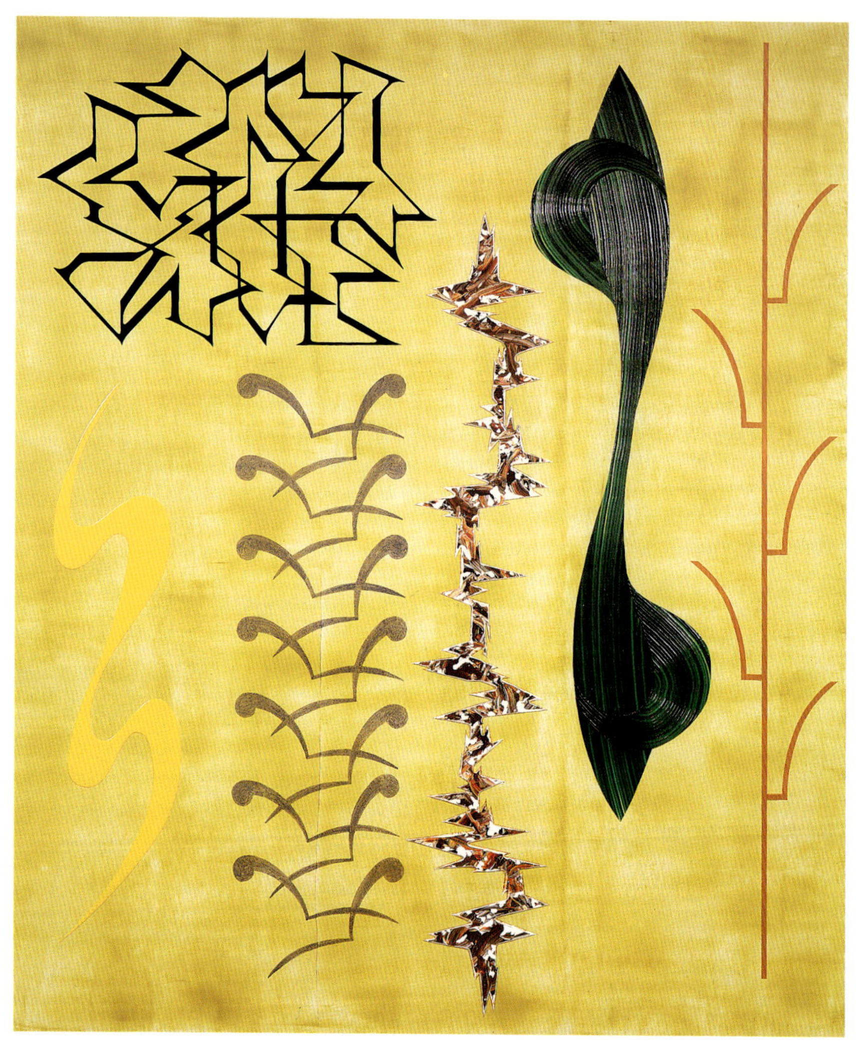

Roland Reiss

Geb and Nut, oil, acrylic and epoxy on panel, 7 x 6'

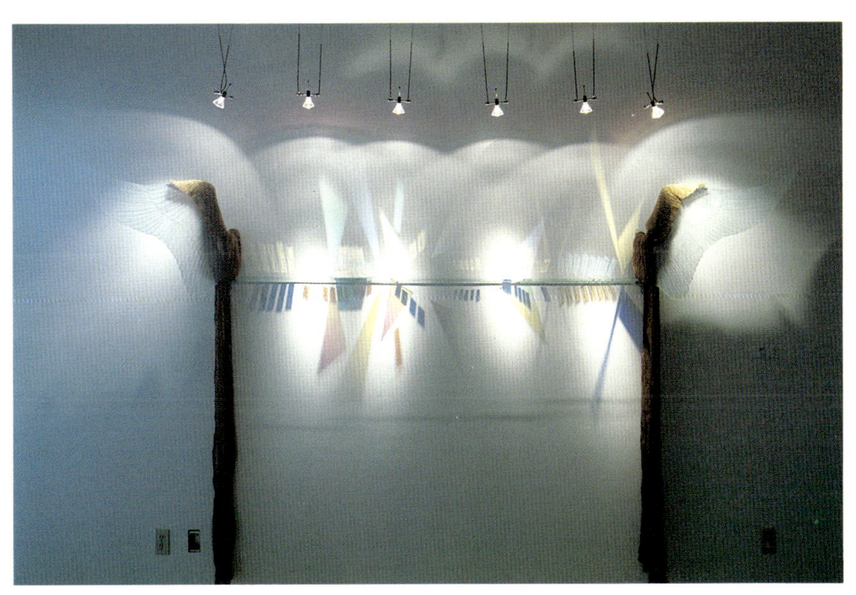

Deanne Sabeck

Wings of Solitude, glass, steel, fabric and projected light, 14 x 8 x 1'

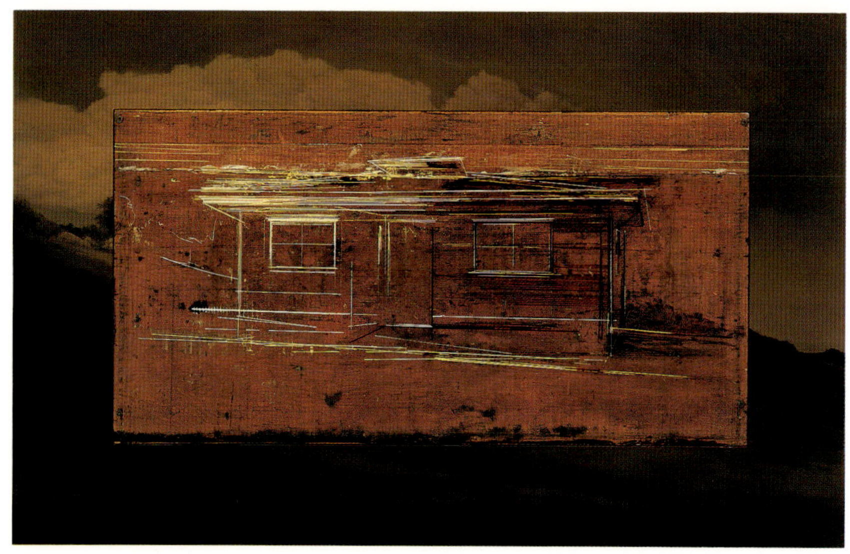

Richard Sedivy

Dropping Down: The Myth of Heracles, or Drawing the Manger, oil, varnish, resin, wood putty and asphalt on wood, 59 x 95". Photo: Douglas M. Parker

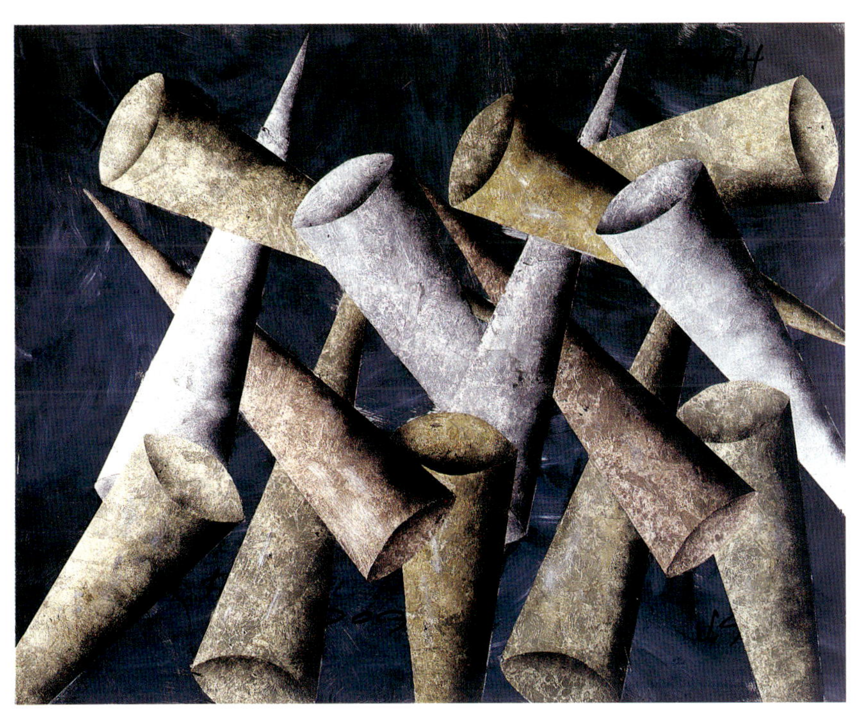

Judy Stabile

Bull, mineral leaf with glass and enamel, 58 x 67". Photo: Tom Randolph

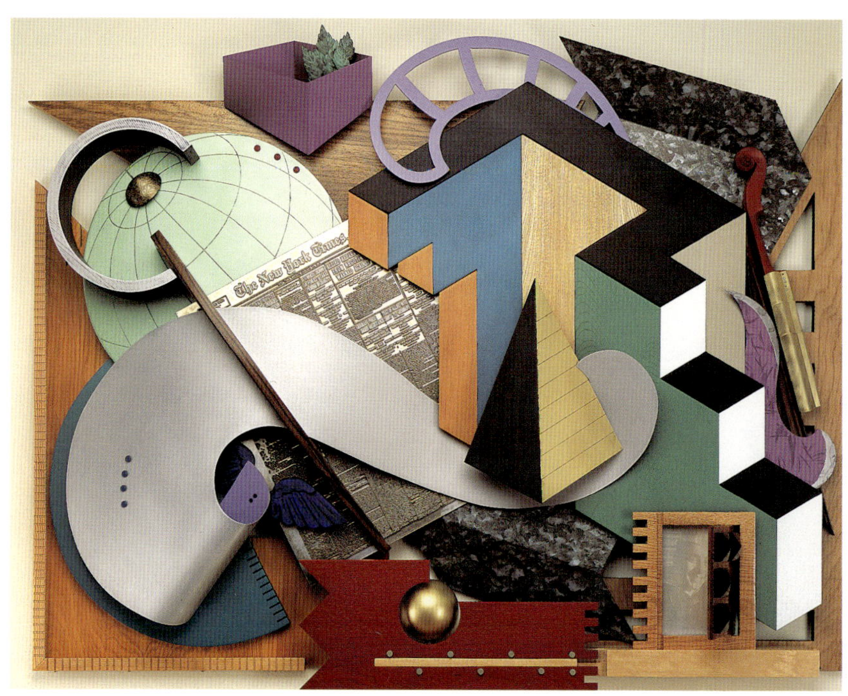

Bob Stimmel

Inquisitive Traveler, painted and natural wood, aluminum, steel, brass and found objects, 40 x 50 x 6"

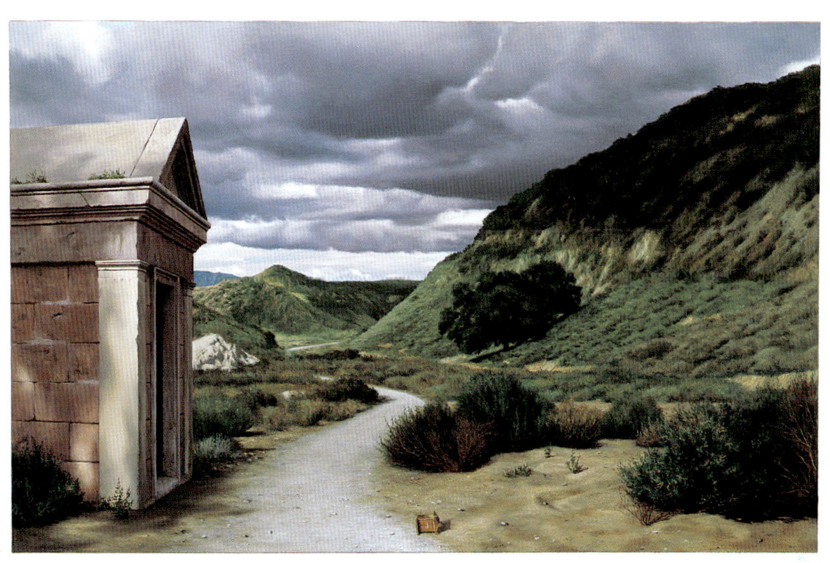

Jon Swihart

Untitled Landscape, oil on panel, 11 x 16". Photo: Gene Ogami

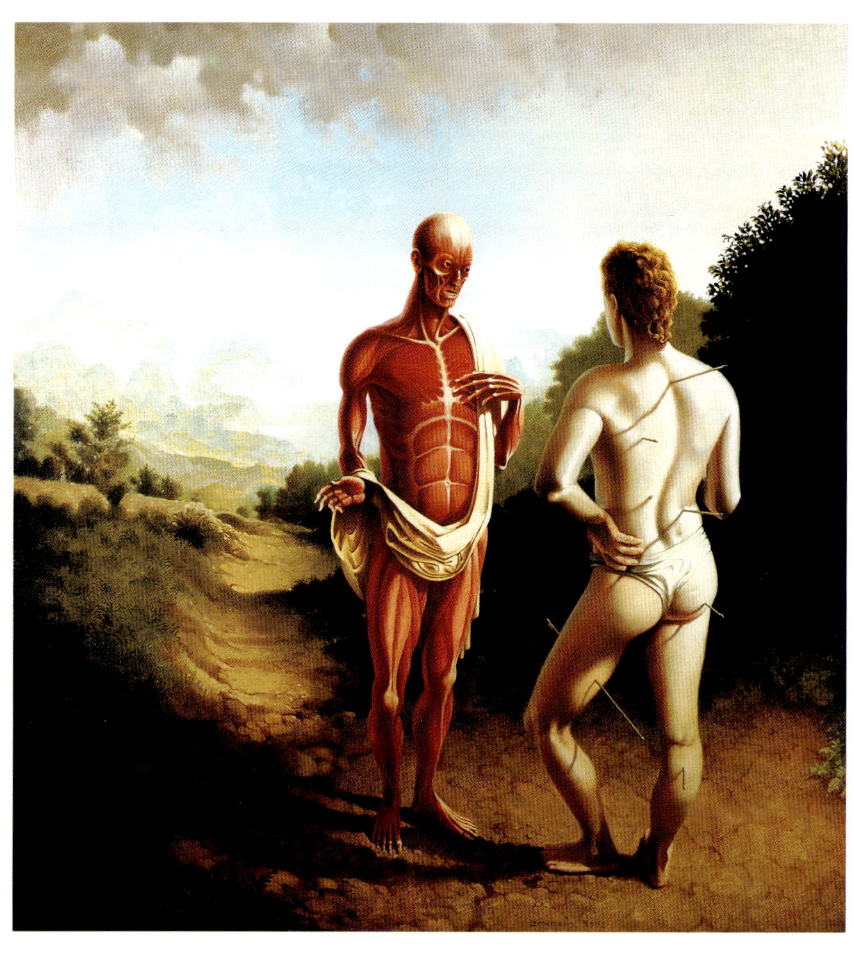

Peter Zokosky

Two Saints, oil on canvas, 39 3/4 x 37"

1301 1301 Franklin Street, Apt 1, Santa Monica, CA 90404 (310) 828-9133

801 North Brand Gallery 801 North Brand Boulevard, Glendale, CA 91203 (818) 549-0315

A Gallery Fine Art 73-580 El Paseo, Palm Desert, CA 92260 (619) 346-8885

A / B Gallery 120 North Robertson Boulevard, #1, Los Angeles, CA 90048 (310) 659-7835

Ace Contemporary Exhibitions 5514 Wilshire Boulevard, Los Angeles, CA 90036 (213) 935-4411

Adamson-Duvannes Galleries 484 South San Vicente Boulevard, Los Angeles, CA 90048 (213) 653-1015

Afro-American Museum 600 State Drive, Exposition Park, Los Angeles, CA 90037 (213) 744-7432

Alitash Kebede Gallery 964 North La Brea Avenue, Los Angeles, CA 90038 (213) 874-6269

Anaheim Museum 241 South Anaheim Boulevard, Anaheim, CA 92805 (714) 778-3301

Angels Gate Cultural Center, The Gate Gallery 3601 South Gaffey Street, San Pedro, CA 90731 (310) 519-0936

Angles Gallery 2230 Main Street, Santa Monica, CA 90405 (310) 396-5019

Antioch University Art Gallery 13274 Fiji Way, 2nd Floor, Marina del Rey, CA 90292 (310) 578-1080

Armory Center for the Arts 145 North Raymond Avenue, Pasadena, CA 91103 (818) 792-5101

Art Center College of Design, Alyce de Roulet Williamson Gallery 1700 Lida Street, Pasadena, CA 91103 (818) 396-2244

Art Collector 4151 Taylor Street, San Diego, CA 92110 (619) 299-3232

Art Dimensions, Inc. 2912 Colorado Avenue, Suite 103, Santa Monica, CA 90404 (310) 828-5532

Artspace Gallery 21800 Oxnard Street, Suite 110, Woodland Hills, CA 91367 (213) 237-1373

Art Store Gallery 7301 West Beverly Boulevard, Los Angeles, CA 90036 (213) 933-9284

Art Works Annex 3720 Main Street, Riverside, CA 92506 (909) 781-6486

Arundel Antiquarian Books, Gallery in the Bookstore 8380 Beverly Boulevard, Los Angeles, CA 90048 (213) 852-9852

B-1 Gallery 2730 Main Street, Santa Monica, CA 90405 (310) 392-9625

Barbara Ackerman 2040 Broadway, Santa Monica, CA 90404 (310) 829-0303

Beyond Baroque 681 Venice Boulevard, Venice, CA 90296 (310) 822-3006

Biola University Art Gallery 13800 Biola Avenue, La Mirada, CA 90639 (310) 903-4807

Bobbie Greenfield Fine Art 74 Market Street, Venice, CA 90291 (310) 392-1771

Boritzer / Gray 1001-B Colorado Avenue, Santa Monica, CA 90401 (310) 394-6652

Galleries & Museums

Bowers Museum of Cultural Art 2002 North Main Street, Santa Ana, CA 92706 (714) 567-3600

Brand Library Art Galleries 1601 West Mountain Street, Glendale, CA 91201 (818) 548-2050

Breeden Gallery 141 South Glassell Street, Orange, CA 92666 (714) 639-3398

Brendan Walter Gallery 1001 Colorado Avenue, Santa Monica, CA 90401 (310) 395-1155

Bronson Fine Arts 1410 2nd Street, Santa Monica, CA 90401 (310) 587-2577

Bryce Bannatyne Gallery 2439 Main Street, Santa Monica, CA 90405 (310) 396-9668

Burnett Miller Gallery 2525 Michigan Avenue, SantaMonica, CA 90404

California Museum of Photography 3824 Main Street, Downtown Pedestrian Mall, Riverside, CA 92501 (909) 784-FOTO

California State University at Fullerton, Art Gallery 800 North State College Boulevard, Fullerton, CA 92634 (714) 773-3262

California State University at Long Beach, University Art Museum 1250 Bellflower Boulevard, Long Beach, CA 90840 (310) 985-5761

California State University at Los Angeles, Fine Arts Gallery 5151 State University Drive, Los Angeles, CA 90032 (213) 343-4023

California State University at Northridge, University Art Gallery 18111 Nordhoff Street, Northridge, CA 91330 (818) 885-2226

California State University at San Bernardino University Art Gallery 5500 University Parkway, San Bernardino, CA 92407 (909) 880-5802

Carl Schlosberg Fine Art 15447 Valley Vista Boulevard, Sherman Oaks, CA 91403 (818) 783-6209

Carnegie Art Museum 424 South C Street, Oxnard, CA (805) 385-8157

Century Gallery, Los Angeles Country Veteran's Memorial Park 13000 Sayre Street, Sylmar, CA 91342 (818) 362-3220

Charles Whitchurch Gallery 5973 Engineer Drive, Huntington Beach, CA 92649 (714) 373-4459

Chim Gregg Art Gallery 159-1 East Main Street, La Puente, CA 91744 (818) 333-8377

Christopher Grimes Gallery 916 Colorado Avenue, Santa Monica, CA 90401 (310) 587-3373

Cirrus Gallery 542 South Alameda Street, Los Angeles, CA 90013 (213) 680-3473

City of Brea Gallery #1 Civic Center Circle, Brea, CA 92621 (714) 990-7730

Claremont Graduate School, East & West Galleries 251 East 10th Street, Claremont, CA 91711 (714) 621-8071

Couturier Gallery 166 North La Brea Avenue, Los Angeles, CA 90036 (213) 933-5557

Craig Krull Gallery 2525 Michigan Avenue, B3, Santa Monica, CA 90404 (310) 828-6410

Cypress College Fine Arts Gallery 9200 Valley View Street, Cypress, CA 90630 (714) 826-5593

Daniel Mayer Gallery 500 Molino Street, #105, Los Angeles, CA 90013 (213) 617-7891

Daniel Saxon Gallery 552 Norwich Drive, Los Angeles, CA 90048 (213) 933-5282

David Zapf Gallery 2400 Kettner Boulevard, San Diego, CA 92101 (619) 232-5004

De Ville Galleries 8751 Melrose Avenue, Los Angeles, CA 90069 (310) 652-0525

del Mano Gallery 11981 San Vicente Boulevard,Los Angeles, CA 90049 (310) 476-8508. Also in Pasadena at 33 E Colorado Boulevard, Pasadena, CA 91105

DeVorzon Gallery 8687 Melrose Avenue, Suite 188, Los Angeles, CA 90069 (310) 659-0555

Dorothy Goldeen Gallery 2224 Main Street, Santa Monica, CA (310) 577-8515

Downey Museum of Art 10419 South Rives Avenue, Downey, CA 90241 (310) 861-0419

Downtown Art Show Space 2349 South Santa Fe Avenue, Los Angeles, CA 90058 (213) 587-6381

ELECTRIC AVENUE - Exhibition and project space **Sharon Truax Fine Art** -Commissions and exhibitions 1625 Electric Avenue, Venice, CA 90291 (310) 396-3162

Ernie Wolfe Gallery 1653 Sawtelle Boulevard, Los Angeles, CA 90025 (310) 478-2960 and 2525 Michigan Avenue, E1, Santa Monica, CA 90404 (310) 582-1555

Ettinger Gallery, AISC 2222 Laguna Canyon Road, Laguna Beach, CA 92651 (714) 497-3309

Fahey / Klein Gallery 148 North La Brea Avenue, Los Angeles, CA 90036 (213) 934-2250

Fine Arts Building Lobby 811 West 7th Street, Los Angeles, CA 90017 (213) 627-4244

Finegood Art Gallery 22622 Vanowen Street, West Hills, CA 91307 (818) 587-3200

First Independent Gallery (FIG) 2022A Broadway, Santa Monica, CA 90404 (310) 829-0345

Food House 2220 Colorado Avenue, Building 4, Room 402, Santa Monica, CA (310) 449-1030

Fullerton Museum Center 301 North Pomona Avenue, Fullerton, CA 92632 (714) 738-6545

G. Ray Hawkins Gallery 908 Colorado Avenue, Santa Monica, CA 90401 (310) 394-5558

Galeria Las Americas 912 East 3rd Street, Suite 402 Los Angeles, CA 90013 (213) 613-1347

Galerie Concréte 201 South Santa Fe Avenue (at 2nd), Loft 209, Los Angeles, CA 90012 (213) 617-7085

Galerie Michael 430 North Rodeo Drive Los Angeles, CA 90210 (310) 273-3377

Gallery 57 204 North Harbor Boulevard, Fullerton, CA 92632 (714) 870-9194

Galleries & Museums

Gallery at 777 777 South Figueroa Street, Los Angeles, CA 90017 (213) 955-5977

Gallery IV 800 Traction Avenue, #9, Los Angeles, CA 90013 (213) 687-8975

Gallery of Functional Art 2525 Michigan Avenue, Santa Monica, CA 90404

Gallery West 107 South Robertson Boulevard, Los Angeles, CA 90048 (310) 271-1145

Garth Clark Gallery 170 South La Brea Avenue, Los Angeles, CA 90036 (213) 939-2189

Gemini G.E.L. 8365 Melrose Avenue, Los Angeles, CA 90069 (213) 651-0513

George J. Doizaki Gallery Japanese American Cultural & Community Center 244 South San Pedro Street, Los Angeles, CA 90012 (213) 628-2725

Getty Center for the History of Art and the Humanities, Seventh Floor Gallery 401 Wilshire Boulevard, Santa Monica, CA 90401 (310) 458-9811, Ext. 4172

Gordon Gallery 1311 Montana Avenue, Santa Monica, CA 90403 (310) 394-6545

Hartog Fine Arts Gallery 6300 Wilshire Boulevard, Los Angeles, CA 90048 (213) 651-2064

Hello Artichoke Gallery 3028 Nebraska Avenue, Santa Monica, CA 90404 (310) 453-6136

Herbert Palmer Gallery 9001 Melrose Avenue, Los Angeles, CA 90069 (310) 278-6407

Heritage Gallery 718 North La Cienega Boulevard, Los Angeles, CA 90069 (310) 652-7738

Hippodrome Gallery 628 Alamitos Avenue, Long Beach, CA 90802 (310) 432-8431

Hunsaker / Schlesinger Gallery 2525 Michigan Avenue, Santa Monica, CA 90404

Huntington Library, Art Collection and Botanical Garden 1151 Oxford Road, San Marino, CA 91108 (818) 405-2100

IMAGO 125 East Tahquitz Canyon Way, Suite 100, Palm Springs, CA 92262 (619) 322-7709

In Collaboration 1219 Olympic Boulevard, Santa Monica, CA 90404 (310) 399-0993

Irvine Museum 18881 Von Karman Avenue (Tower 17), 12th Floor, Irvine, CA 92715 (714) 476-0294

Ituralde Gallery 154 North La Brea Avenue, Los Angeles, CA 90036 (213) 937-4267

J. Paul Getty Museum 17985 Pacific Coast Highway, Malibu, CA 90265 (310) 459-7611 Parking registration necessary for admittance to the museum (310) 458-2003 (parking)

Jack Rutberg Fine Arts 357 North La Brea Avenue, Los Angeles, CA 90036 (213) 938-5222

James Corcoran Gallery (310) 451-4666

Jan Abrams 9002 Melrose Avenue, Los Angeles, CA 90069 (310) 278-8790

Jan Baum Gallery 170 South La Brea Avenue, Los Angeles, CA 90036 (213) 932-0170

Jan Kesner Gallery 164 North La Brea Avenue, Los Angeles, CA 90036 (213) 938-6834

Jane Moufflet Gallery 8840 Beverly Boulevard, Los Angeles, CA 90048 (310) 275-3629

Japanese American National Museum 369 East 1st Street, Los Angeles, CA 90012 (213) 625-0414

John Thomas Gallery 1831 Colorado Avenue, Santa Monica, CA 90404 (310) 396-6096

Julie Rico Gallery 2623 Main Street, Santa Monica, CA 90405 (310) 399-1177

Junior Arts Center Gallery 4814 Hollywood Boulevard, Los Angeles, CA 90027 (213) 485-4474

Keesling Gallery 1109 1/2 Montana Avenue, Santa Monica, CA 90403 (310) 451-7714

Kim Light Gallery 126 North La Brea Avenue, Los Angeles, CA 90036 (213) 933-9816

Kiyo Higashi Gallery 8332 Melrose Avenue, Los Angeles, CA 90069 (213) 655-2482

Kohn Turner Gallery 9006 Melrose Avenue, Los Angeles, CA 90069 (310) 271-4453

Koplin Gallery 1438 9th Street, Santa Monica, CA 90401 (310) 319-9956

L.A. Artcore Center 420 East 3rd Street, Suite 110, Los Angeles, CA 90021 **Brewery Annex** 650A South Avenue 21, Los Angeles, CA, 90031 (213) 617-3274

L.A. Louver 55 North Venice Boulevard and 77 Market Street, Venice, CA 90291 (310) 822-4955

La Sierra University, Brandstater Gallery 4700 Pierce Street, Riverside, CA 92515 (909) 785-2959

Laguna Art Museum 307 Cliff, Laguna Beach, CA 92651 (714) 494-6531

Landau/20th Century Art (310) 474-5155

Lannan Foundation 5401 McConnell Avenue, Los Angeles, CA 90066 (310) 306-1004

Latin American Masters 264 North Beverly Drive, Beverly Hills, CA 90210 (310) 271-4847

Leslie Sacks Fine Art 11640 San Vicente Boulevard, Los Angeles, CA 90049 (310) 820-9448

Linda Moore Gallery 1611 West Lewis, San Diego, CA 92103 (619) 260-1101

Long Beach City College Art Gallery 4901 East Carson Street, Long Beach, CA 90808 (310) 420-4317

Long Beach Museum of Art 2300 East Ocean Boulevard, Long Beach, CA 90803 (310) 439-2119

Los Angeles Art Association 825 North La Cienega Boulevard, Los Angeles, CA 90069 (310) 652-8272

Los Angeles Center for Photographic Studies (LACPS) 6518 Hollywood Boulevard, Los Angeles, CA (213) 482-3566

Los Angeles City College Art Gallery, Da Vinci Hall 855 North Vermont Avenue, Los Angeles, CA 90029 (213) 953-4220

Los Angeles Contemporary Exhibitions (LACE) 6522 Hollywood Boulevard, Los Angeles, CA 90028 (213) 957-1777

Los Angeles County Museum of Art (LACMA) 5905 Wilshire Boulevard, Los Angeles, CA 90036 (213) 857-6111

Los Angeles Municipal Art Gallery 4804 Hollywood Boulevard, Los Angeles, CA 90027 (213) 485-4581

Louis Newman Galleries 322 North Beverly Drive Beverly Hills, CA 90210 (310) 278-6311

Loyola Marymount University, Laband Gallery 7101 West 80th Street, Los Angeles, CA 90045 (310) 338-2880

Manny Silverman Gallery 619 North Almont Drive, Los Angeles, CA 90069 (310) 659-8256

Margo Leavin Gallery 812 North Robertson Boulevard, Los Angeles, CA 90069 (310) 273-0603

Mark Moore 2032-A Broadway, Santa Monica, CA 90404 (310) 453-3031

Mendenhall Gallery 30 Smith Alley (located in One Colorado), Pasadena, CA 91103 (818) 792-0162

Merging One Gallery 1547 6th Street, Santa Monica, CA 90401 (310) 395-0033

Michael Hittleman Gallery 8797 Beverly Boulevard, #302 Los Angeles, CA 90048 (213) 655-5364

Michael Kizhner Fine Art 746 North La Cienega Boulevard, Los Angeles, CA 90069 (310) 659-5222

Modern Art Gallery 3466 West 8th Street, Los Angeles, CA 90005 (213) 487-2565

Morosstudio Art Gallery 120 Broadway, Suite 103, Santa Monica, CA 90401 (310) 458-4406

Mount San Antonio College Art Gallery 1100 North Grand Avenue, Walnut, CA 91789 (909) 594-5611 x 4326

Museum of African American Art 4005 S. Crenshaw Boulevard, May Company, Third Floor, Los Angeles, CA (213) 294-7071

Museum of Contemporary Art (MOCA) 250 S. Grand Avenue, Los Angeles, CA 90012 (213) 62-MOCA-2

Museum of Contemporary Art, San Diego 1001 Kettner Boulevard, San Diego, CA 92101 (619) 234-1001

Museum of Contemporary Art, San Diego 700 Prospect, La Jolla 92037 (619) 454-3541 Closed for renovation/expansion until 1996.

Neal Menzies 170 South La Brea Avenue, Los Angeles, CA 90036 (213) 965-1274

Nemiroff Deutsch Fine Art 2444 Wilshire Boulevard, Suite 508, Santa Monica, CA 90403 (310) 315-5400

New Canyon Gallery 129 South Topanga Canyon Boulevard, Topanga, CA 90290 (310) 455-3923

Newport Harbor Art Museum 850 San Clemente Drive, Newport Beach, CA 92660 (714) 759-1122

Newspace 5241 Melrose Avenue, Los Angeles, CA 90038 (213) 469-9353

Norton Simon Museum 441 West Colorado Boulevard, Pasadena, CA 91105 (818) 449-6840

Occidental College, Weingart and Coons Galleries 1600 Campus Road, Los Angeles, CA 90041 (213) 259-2749

Orange County Center for Contemporary Art (OCCCA) 3621 West MacArthur Boulevard, #111 Santa Ana, CA 92704 (714) 549-4989

Orlando Gallery 14553 Ventura Boulevard, Sherman Oaks, CA 91403 (818) 789-6012

Otis School of Art & Design Gallery 2401 Wilshire Boulevard, Los Angeles, CA 90057 (213) 251-0555

Ovsey Gallery 170 South La Brea Avenue, Los Angeles, CA 90036 (213) 935-1883

Pacific Asia Museum 46 North Los Robles Avenue, Pasadena, CA 91101 (818) 449-2741

Palladio Gallery 5750 Wilshire Boulevard, Suite 180, Los Angeles, CA 90036 (213) 933-4025

Palm Springs Desert Museum 101 Museum Drive, Palm Springs, CA 92262 (619) 322-0189

Palos Verdes Art Center 5504 West Crestridge Road, Rancho Palos Verde, CA 90274 (310) 541-2479

Parnas Gallery 1547 10th Street, Santa Monica, CA 90401 (310) 458-6335

Pasadena City College Art Gallery 1570 East Colorado Boulevard, Pasadena, CA 91105 (818) 585-7238

Pascal de Sarthe Gallery 640 North La Peer Drive, Los Angeles, CA 90069 (310) 289-1012

Patricia Correia Gallery 2525 Michigan Avenue, E2, Santa Monica, CA 90404 (310) 314-2626

Patricia Faure Gallery 2525 Michigan Avenue, Santa Monica, CA 90404

Patricia Shea Gallery 2042 Broadway, Santa Monica, CA 90404 (310) 452-4210

Paul Kopeikin Gallery 170 South La Brea Avenue, Los Angeles, CA 90038 (213) 937-0765

Pax Gallery 1411 Fifth St. (Mezzanine), Santa Monica, CA 90401 (310) 395-9919

Pepperdine University, Frederick R. Weissman Museum 24255 Pacific Coast Highway, Malibu, CA 90265 (310) 456-4851

Peter Fetterman Gallery 2525 Michigan Avenue, A7, Santa Monica, CA 90404 (310) 453-6463

Pheromone 8642 Melrose Avenue, Suite 101, Los Angeles, CA 90069 (310) 659-5075

Photo Impact Gallery 931 North Citrus Avenue, Los Angeles, CA 90038 (213) 461-0141

Pierce College Art Gallery 6201 Winnetka Avenue, Woodland Hills, CA 91371 (818) 719-6498

Platt Gallery, University of Judaism 15600 Mulholland Drive, Los Angeles, CA 90077 (310) 476-9777, ext 276

Galleries & Museums

Porter Randall Gallery 5624 La Jolla Boulevard, La Jolla, CA 92037 (619) 551-8884

Posner Fine Art 1119 Montana Avenue, Santa Monica, CA, 90403 (310) 260-8858

Quint Gallery 7447 Girard Avenue, La Jolla, CA 92037 (619) 454-3409

Rachele Lozzi Gallery 930 Wilshire Boulevard, Los Angeles Hilton Towers, Los Angeles, CA 90017 (213) 612-3965

Rancho Santiago College Art Gallery 17th at Bristol, Santa Ana, CA 92706 (714) 564-5615

Random Gallery 6040 North Figueroa Street, Los Angeles, CA 90042 (213) 550-8000

Regent Projects 629 Almont Drive, Los Angeles, CA 90069 (310) 276-5424

Remba Gallery 464 North Robertson Boulevard, West Hollywood, CA 90048 (310) 657-1101

Richard Telles Fine Art 7380 Beverly Boulevard, Los Angeles, CA 90036 (213) 965-5578

Rio Hondo College Art Gallery 3600 Workman Mill Road, Whittier, CA 90068

Riverside Art Museum 3425 7th Avenue, Riverside, CA 92501 (909) 684-7111

Riverside College Art Gallery 4800 Magnolia Avenue, Riverside, CA 92506 (909) 684-3240, x 540

Ro Snell Gallery 926 Chapala Street, Santa Barbara, CA 93101 (805) 966-0903

Robert Berman Gallery 2044 Broadway, and 2525 Michigan Avenue, C2, Santa Monica, CA 90404 (310) 453-9195

Roberts Art Gallery 601 Pico Boulevard, Santa Monica, CA 90405 (310) 395-3204, Ext. 508

Rosamund Felsen Gallery 8525 Santa Monica Boulevard, Los Angeles, CA 90069 (310) 652-9172

Rose City Gallery 474 South Arroyo Parkway, Pasadena, CA 91105 (818) 793-9539

Roy G. Biv Gallery 146 North Palm Canyon Drive, Palm Springs, CA 92262 (619) 325-8535

Ruth Bachofner Gallery 2046 Broadway, Santa Monica, CA 90404 (310) 829-3300

Ruth Bloom Gallery 2036 Broadway, Santa Monica, CA 90404 (310) 399-2170

Ruth Chandler Williamson Gallery, Scripps College 1030 Columbia Avenue, Claremont, CA 91711 (909) 621-8000 x 3517

Saddleback College Art Gallery 28000 Marguerite Parkway, Mission Viejo, CA 92692 (714) 582-4924

Sam Francis Gallery, Crossroads School for Arts and Sciences 1714 21st Street, Santa Monica, CA 90404 (310) 829-7391

San Diego Museum of Art Balboa Park, San Diego, CA 92101 (619) 232-7931

Santa Barbara Contemporary Arts Forum 653 Paseo Nuevo, Santa Barbara, CA 93101 (805) 966-5373

Santa Barbara Museum of Art 1130 State Street, Santa Barbara, CA 93103 (805) 963-4364

Santa Monica College Art Gallery 1900 Pico Boulevard, Santa Monica, CA 90405 (310) 452-9231

Santa Monica Heritage Museum 2612 Main Street, Santa Monica, CA 90405 (310) 392-8537

Santa Monica Museum of Art 2437 Main Street, Santa Monica, CA 90405 (310) 399-0433

Sarah Bain Gallery 1112 Brea Mall, Brea, CA 92621 (714) 257-1440

Sculpture Placement Center 2525 Michigan Avenue, Santa Monica, CA 90404

Self Help Graphics and Art, Galeria Otra Vez 3802 Brooklyn Avenue, Los Angeles, CA 90063 (213) 264-1259

Senior Eye Gallery, Palmcrest House 3501 Cedar Avenue, Long Beach, CA 90807 (310) 595-4551

Severin Wunderman Museum 3 Mason, Irvine, CA 92718 (714) 472-1138

Sherry Frumkin Gallery 2525 Michigan Avenue, Santa Monica, CA 90404 (310) 285-9370

Sho-En 15090 Sho-En Lane, Ramona, CA 92065 (619) 789-7079

Shoshana Wayne Gallery 2525 Michigan Avenue, Santa Monica, CA 90404 (310) 453-7535

Site Gallery at the Roosevelt Building 719 West 7th Street, Los Angeles, CA 90017 (213) 629-4532

Soma Gallery 343 Fourth Avenue, San Diego, CA 92101 (619) 232-3955

Space Gallery 6015 Santa Monica Boulevard, Los Angeles, CA (213) 461-8166

Stephen Cohen 7466 Beverly Boulevard, Los Angeles, CA 90036 (213) 937-5525

Studio Raid Gallery 7378 Beverly Boulevard, Los Angeles, CA 90036 (213) 939-8085

Sue Spaid Fine Art 7454 1/2 Beverly Boulevard, Los Angeles, CA 90036 (213) 935-6153

Susan Spiritus Gallery 1870-A Harbor Boulevard, #212, Costa Mesa, CA 92627 (714) 548-7558

Sylvia White 2022 B Broadway, Santa Monica, CA 90404 (310) 828-6200

T. Heritage Gallery 1062 Westwood Boulevard, Los Angeles, CA 90024 (310) 839-5058

Tamara Bane Gallery 8025 Melrose Avenue, Los Angeles, CA 90046 (213) 651-1400

Tasende Gallery 820 Prospect Street, La Jolla, CA 92037 (619) 454-3691

Tatistcheff / Rogers 2042 A Broadway, Santa Monica, CA 90404 (310) 449-1240

Third World Art Exchange 2016 North Hillhurst Avenue, Los Angeles, CA 90027 (213) 666-9357

Thomas Babeor Gallery 7470 Girard Avenue La Jolla, CA 92037 (619) 454-0345

Thomas Solomon's Garage 928 North Fairfax Los Angeles, CA 90046 (213) 654-4731

Tobey C. Moss Gallery 7321 Beverly Boulevard, Los Angeles, CA 90036 (213) 933-5523

Tomlin-Acheson Fine Art 216 Pier Avenue, Santa Monica, CA 90405 (310) 396-1592

Tortue Gallery 2917 Santa Monica Boulevard, Santa Monica, CA 90404 (310) 828-8878

Track 16 Gallery 2525 Michigan Avenue, Santa Monica CA, 90404

Turner / Krull Gallery 9006 Melrose Avenue, Los Angeles, CA 90069 (310) 271-1536

University of California at Riverside, University Art Gallery Riverside, CA 92521 (909) 787-3755

University of California at Irvine, Fine Art Gallery UC Irvine, Irvine, CA 92717 (714) 856-66120

University of California at Santa Barbara, University Art Museum UC Santa Barbara, Santa Barbara, CA 93106 (619) 961-2951

UCLA at the Armand Hammer Museum of Art and Cultural Center 10899 Wilshire Boulevard, Los Angeles, CA 90024 (310) 443-7000

University of California at Los Angeles (UCLA) Wight Art Gallery 405 Hilgard Avenue, Los Angeles, CA 90024 (310) 825-1461

University of Southern California - Fisher Gallery 823 Exposition Boulevard, Los Angeles, CA 90089 (213) 740-4561

University Union Exhibit Gallery, CAL Poly Pomona 3801 West Temple Avenue, Building 35, Pomona, CA 91768 (909) 869-2850

Valerie Miller Fine Art 73-100 El Paseo, Palm Desert, CA 92260 (619) 773-4483

Vincent Price Gallery, East Los Angeles College 1301 Avenida Cesar Chavez, Monterey Park, CA 91754 (213) 265- 8841

Watts Towers Art Center 1727 East 107th Street, Los Angeles, CA 90002 (213) 847-4646

Wenger Gallery 1414 Sixth Street, Santa Monica, CA 90401 (310) 451-8988

Whittier College, Mendenhall Art Gallery 13406 Philadelphia Street, Whittier, CA 90608 (310) 907-4200 X 4311

Whittier Museum 6755 Newlin Avenue, Whittier, CA 90601 (310) 945-3871

William Reach LA Photography Center 412 South Park View, Los Angeles, CA 90057 (213) 383-7342

William Turner Gallery 69 Market Street, Venice, CA 90291 (310) 392-8399

Woodbury University Art Gallery 7500 Glenoaks Boulevard, Burbank, CA 91510 (818) 767-0888

X-ibit Gallery 102 Robinson Street, Los Angeles, CA 90026 (213) 380-1500

Zeneta Kertisz-Art 1319 Abbot Kinney Boulevard, Venice, CA 90291 (310) 399-8188

Artist Index

The page numbers in bold face refer to color illustrations

Index by Media

The page numbers in bold face refer to color illustrations

Notes

Notes

Notes